John William Cunliffe

The influence of seneca on Elizabethan tragedy; An essay

John William Cunliffe

The influence of seneca on Elizabethan tragedy; An essay

ISBN/EAN: 9783337809607

Printed in Europe, USA, Canada, Australia, Japan

Cover: Foto ©ninafisch / pixelio.de

More available books at **www.hansebooks.com**

THE
INFLUENCE OF SENECA
ON
ELIZABETHAN TRAGEDY

AN ESSAY

BY

JOHN W. CUNLIFFE, D.Lit., M.A.,

Late Berkeley Fellow of the Owens College, Manchester.

London
MACMILLAN AND CO.
AND NEW YORK
1893

ANASTATIC REPRINT 1907.
G.E. STECHERT & C°., NEW YORK.

PREFACE.

This investigation was suggested to me while attending Dr. Ward's English Literature Lectures at the Owens College in the Session 1885-6; and after going through the degree courses on which I was then engaged, I gave the subject such attention as was at my command. It would probably have been a long time before I arrived at results worthy, even in my own opinion, of publication, but for my appointment to a Bishop Berkeley Fellowship at the College, which has enabled me to give undivided attention to the inquiry for the last two years. I have to thank Dr. Ward for help and encouragement in addition to the original suggestion of the subject of investigation; indeed, I should have liked to dedicate this little work to him as its "only begetter," but that I hesitate to connect his name with faults which are all my own. I am also under obligations to Dr. Wilkins, to Mr. Elton, Lecturer in English Literature, and to other members of the staff of the Owens College for their kindly interest in my work and ready response to any appeal on questions of scholarship in connection with a subject which has points of contact with many branches of ancient and modern literature.

In giving the results of the investigation, I have endeavoured to keep as closely as possible to the main lines of an inquiry which offers unusual temptations to digression. I may, however, be permitted to state here, very shortly, my opinion on some of the points I have declined to discuss in the essay. The identity of the author of the tragedies with Seneca the philosopher seems to me sufficiently established; but the *Octavia* and the *Hercules Oetaeus* are clearly not his, and there is something to be said against the *Thebais* and the *Agamemnon*. As to the Shaksperean controversies referred to, I accept Miss Jane Lee's theory as to the authorship of Parts II and III of *Henry VI*, and it seems to me not unlikely that in *Richard III* Shakspere made use of a previous play. The arguments lately brought forward by Dr. Sarrazin in *Anglia*, coupled with the recently discovered fact that Kyd's father was a scrivener, convince me that Kyd is the tragedian attacked by Nash in the Preface to Greene's *Menaphon*, and therefore the author of the old *Hamlet* upon which Shakspere founded his immortal tragedy. Having given considerable attention to this famous controversy, I was tempted to add another appendix dealing with Nash's allusions and the developement of the *Hamlet* tragedy, but in the end I deemed it wiser not to wander so far from the path on which I had set out.

It remains to be added that the essay was submitted to the examiners for the Doctorate of Literature in the University of London, and accepted by them as a sufficient qualification for the degree.

JOHN W. CUNLIFFE.

January, 1893.

THE INFLUENCE OF SENECA ON ELIZABETHAN[1] TRAGEDY.

The influence of Seneca (or, to speak more correctly, of the tragedies ascribed to him) upon the Elizabethan drama is so plainly marked that no competent historian of our literature could fail to notice it. The translations of Seneca and their connection with the beginnings of the regular drama in England have been referred to by Warton, by Collier, and by Dr. Ward; and Mr. J. A. Symonds has an admirable review of the whole subject.[2] Indeed, the obligations of our early dramatists to Seneca did not escape the attention of contemporary critics. Writing "to the Gentlemen Students of both Universities" in the preface to Greene's *Menaphon*, (pub. 1589), Thomas Nash inveighs in his usual lively style against *Thomas Nash.* "the seruile imitation of vain-glorious tragoedians........ who (mounted on the stage of arrogance) think to out-braue better pens with the swelling bumbast of a bragging blanke verse." After a violent outburst of contemptuous

---

[1] I have used the term "Elizabethan" in its broad literary meaning rather than in the strict historical sense. It seems to me more expressive, as well as more convenient, than the cumbrous "Elizabetho-Jacobæan," or even the less objectionable term, "pre-Restoration." The drama was one in spirit throughout the three reigns, and exhibits only continuous stages of developement from the first plays of Lyly and Marlowe to the last plays of Shirley.

[2] *Shakspere's Predecessors in the English Drama*, Chapter VI.

indignation, he threatens "to leaue these to the mercie of their mother tongue, that feed on nought but the crummes that fal from the translators trencher;" but he soon resolves to "turne back to his first text; and talke a little in friendship with a few of our triuiall translators." "It is," he says, "a common practise now a daies amongst a sort of shifting companions, that runne through euery arte and thriue by none, to leaue the trade of *Nouerint* whereto they were borne, and busie themselues with the indeuors of Art, that could scarcelie latinize their necke-verse if they should haue neede; yet English *Seneca* read by candle light yeeldes manie good sentences, as *Bloud is a begger*, and so foorth: and if you intreate him faire in a frostie morning, he will affoord you whole *Hamlets*, I should say handfulls of tragical speaches. But ô griefe! *tempus edax rerum*, what's that will last alwaies? The sea exhaled by droppes will in continuance be drie, and *Seneca* let blood line by line and page by page, at length must needes die to our stage........" The whole passage is one of great interest as a contemporary criticism of the dramatic models of the time, but it is too long for full quotation. I must content myself with drawing attention to the reference to the translation of Seneca, which is also mentioned by Ascham in *The Scholemaster* (1570), by Arthur Hall in the preface to his *Homer* (1581), by William Webbe in his *Discourse of English Poetrie* (1586), and by Francis Meres in *Palladis Tamia* (1598). This translation, which held a high place in the esteem of contemporary critics, and, according to Nash, was laid under heavy contribution by the dramatists, merits careful examination, because of its close and important connection with the subject of this essay.

The translation of Seneca's "Tenne Tragedies" appeared as a whole in 1581, but all the plays composing the volume had been previously published, with the exception of the fragmentary *Thebais*. The *Troas* had been printed in 1559, the *Thyestes* in 1560, the *Hercules Furens* in 1561, all from the pen of Jasper Heywood; the *Oedipus* was translated by Alexander Nevyle in 1560 and published in 1563; the *Octavia* was done by Thomas Nuce in 1562 and printed in 1566, the *Medea* and *Agamemnon* by John Studley appearing in the same year; the *Hippolytus* was licensed to Henry Denham in 1556-7, and was doubtless printed, though no copy of this edition is known; the *Thebais* was added in 1581 by Thomas Newton, the editor of the whole, for the sake of completeness.

The translation seems to have been intended, at least in part, for dramatic representation. Nevyle, in his preface to the *Oedipus*, says his translation was not at first meant for publication, "but onely to satisfy the instant requests of a few my familiar frends, who thought to haue put it to the very same vse, that *Seneca* himselfe in his Inuention pretended: Which was by the tragicall and Pompous showe upon Stage, to admonish all men....." The translator of the *Troas* seems to have had the same end in view, as may be gathered from the last line of the chorus at the end of Act II :—

And now (good Ladies) heare what shall be done.

Taken as a whole the translation is generally close, but not always correct. Difficult passages are rendered in a literal and often meaningless way, and sometimes slurred over or omitted altogether. Occasionally the translator expands a familiar reflection, or inserts a few lines of his own. Jasper Heywood added a long soliloquy to the *Thyestes*, and made in the *Troas* a considerable number of alterations, which he details in the preface to that tragedy; his additions are affected to some extent by the tastes of his time, but are for the most part after the style of the original, the third Chorus in Heywood's *Troas* being borrowed from the third Chorus in Seneca's *Hippolytus*. There is an interesting insertion in the speech of Phaedra on folio 73 (And sith that I.....) by Studley, who also altered the first Chorus in the *Medea* out of all semblance of translation, and added to the *Agamemnon* a long speech by Eurybates. Studley also made omissions and additions of some interest in the *Hercules Oetaeus*. In Nevyle's *Oedipus* the first Chorus is considerably shortened, the second is left out altogether, and the third and fourth bear little or no resemblance to the original. Nevyle apologises for thus " adding and subtracting at pleasure," and in the preface to the *Troas* Heywood excuses himself on the ground that the author's mind is " in many places verye harde and doubtfull, and the worke much corrupt by the default of euil printed Bookes." Doubtless everyone of the translators would be able to make with truth the avowal of the editor, Newton, " Yet this dare I saye, I haue deliuered myne Authors meaning with as much perspicuity, as so meane a Scholler, out of so meane a stoare, in so smal a time, and vpon so short a warning was well able to performe;" and when we take into consideration the state of the text at that day, and the youth of some of the authors (Nevyle was only 15), the translation seems a very creditable, and even an admirable performance. There is every evidence that it was highly esteemed and extensively used; but I have been unable to confirm Nash's taunt that playwrights ignorant of Latin found in English *Seneca*, not merely "manie good sentences," but "whole *Hamlets*, I should say handfulls of tragical speaches." A large and important chapter of Shaksperean controversy centres in this reference by Nash in 1589 to an earlier *Hamlet*, which is also referred to in Lodge's *Wits miserie, and the Worlds madnesse, discovering the Devils incarnat of this Age* (1596). One of these devils is described as "a foule lubber, who........looks as pale as the visard of the ghost, which cried so miserally at the theator, like an oisterwife, *Hamlet reuenge.*" We find from Henslowe's *Diary* that a *Hamlet* had been acted at Newington on June 9th, 1594, and there is also a reference by Tucca in Dekker's *Satiromastix* (1602). This earlier *Hamlet* doubtless formed the foundation for Shakspere's tragedy as we have it, but the text of 1603-4 offers no confirmation for Nash's sneers, and the German *Hamlet* published by Mr. Cohn does not help us. Doubtless in the old *Hamlet*, if we had it, we should be able to discover the "good sentences" and "tragical speaches" borrowed by the author from English *Seneca*; and in many other old plays now lost we might find evidence in

The Earlier Hamlet.

support of Nash's criticisms. The learned dramatists of the Inns of Court and the popular playwrights of a later date who borrowed from Seneca seem to have gone to the Latin text, and their version is often more accurate, as well as more elegant, than the rendering of the professed translators. Of course the dramatists who used Seneca's lines without acknowledgment would not be likely to reveal their indebtedness to the English version, if they could avoid it; and there can be little doubt that the translation would be extensively used in conjunction with the original by those who had but "small Latin," and were glad to take advantage of what help they could get to puzzle out Seneca's aphoristic obscurities and far-fetched allusions. The translation must also have had considerable effect in spreading a general knowledge of Seneca's form, style, and manner, the character of his subjects, and the leading ideas of his philosophical teaching as contained in the tragedies.

cent neglect of Seneca.

The translation of 1581 is further remarkable as the only complete version of Seneca's tragedies in the English language. Sir Edward Sherburne in 1701 published a translation of the *Medea*, the *Hippolytus*, and the *Troas*, and odd plays were printed by other translators;[1] but the issue of 1581 still remains the first and only English translation of the ten tragedies. For many years past, Seneca has been treated, at any rate in England,

---

[1] In the Bodleian Library there is a translation from the *Hercules Oetaeus* by Queen Elizabeth.

with a contemptuous neglect contrasting strangely with
the high esteem in which he was once held. I suppose
no one nowadays would think of upholding the judgement
of Scaliger: "Senecam nullo Graecorum maie tatem
inferiorem existimo, cultu vero ac nitore, etiam Euripide
maiorem." Few critics would pin their faith even to the
more moderate claim of Muretus: "Est profecto poeta
ille praeclarior et uetusti sermonis diligentior quam quidam
inepte fastidiosi suspicantur.". But altogether apart from
his intrinsic merits, Seneca held such a prominent place *Seneca and European nascence.*
in the Revival of Learning in Europe, and exercised such
a great influence on the developement of the modern
drama, that the study of his tragedies is of the utmost
importance. When Alberto Mussato gave new life to the
European drama at the beginning of the fourteenth century, though his subjects were taken from modern history,
his model, both in style and metre, was Seneca. At a
later date Italian tragedy, to use the words of Klein,[1]
"indeed exchanged Mussato's Latin for the vulgar tongue;
but only to again force this too into the Senecan buskin."
"With every subsequent tragedy of the sixteenth century," Klein says later, "with every step we fall deeper
and deeper into the savagery.......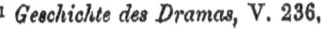of the tragedy of Seneca."
The influence of Seneca runs through Italian tragedy from
Mussato right down to Alfieri; and, to again quote Klein,
through Seneca "Euripidean tragedy leavened the dramatic poetry of every cultured nation in Europe through
all the centuries, while Aeschylus and Sophocles fed the
worms in the libraries." As to the French drama, it will

---

[1] *Geschichte des Dramas*, V. 236.

be enough to give the statement of Mr. George Saintsbury[1] that Seneca took captive "the whole drama of France, from Jodelle, through Garnier and Montchrestien and even Hardy, through Corneille and Racine and Voltaire, leaving his traces even on Victor Hugo." The "Primeras Tragedias Espanõles" of Geronymo Bermudez, published at Madrid in 1577, bear traces of Seneca's influence; and the "Nueva Idea de la Tragedia Antigua" of Gonzalez de Salas (Madrid, 1633) contains a translation of the *Troas;* but the main current of the Spanish drama seems to have been little affected by classical influence. The German dramatist Gryphius took Seneca as his model; and as early as 1540-3 the Scotch scholar, Buchanan, had written in Seneca's manner a Latin tragedy, *Jephthaes,* which, after being acted by the students of Bordeaux, was printed in 1554, and became very popular. It is commended by Ascham in *The Scholemaster,* and by R. Wilmott in his preface to the revised edition of *Tancred and Gismund* (1592). Latin imitations of Seneca, as well as the original plays, were acted at the Universities.[2]

[1] In a Preliminary Note to Vol. III. of Dr. Grosart's *Complete Works of Samuel Daniel.*

[2] Knight mentions in a note on *Hamlet* that in Braun's *Civitates* (1575) there is a Latin memoir prefixed to a map of Cambridge, recording that the fables of Seneca were performed by the students "with elegance, magnificence, dignity of action, and propriety of voice and countenance." Gager's *Meleager,* a Latin tragedy in the form of Seneca and described by the author as "Panniculus Hippolyto Senecae Tragaediae assutus," was acted at Christ Church, Oxford, before Lord Leicester, Sir Philip Sidney, and others in 1581, according to Mr. Fleay's *Chronicle of the English Drama,* I. 236. It was printed at Oxford in 1592, and the author or publisher apparently fixes the date of composition at 1591.

Seneca influenced English tragedy through both Italian and French literature. Gascoigne's *Jocasta* (1566) is an adaptation of the *Phoenissae* of Euripides, cast into the form of Seneca, and taken from Ludovico Dolce, the Italian translator of Seneca. Kyd, the author of *The Spanish Tragedy*, translated Garnier's *Cornelia*, a close copy of Seneca's style (pub. 1594); and Garnier's *Antonius* was done into English by the Countess of Pembroke in 1590 and printed in 1592. But we need not seek for the influence of Seneca on the English drama through these indirect channels. The direct influence was of much greater extent and importance. Seneca was held in no less esteem in England than on the Continent. Without going back to Chaucer[1] and Lydgate, it is worthy of note that in the early days of the English Renascence, in Skelton's *Garlande of Laurell* (1523), "Senek full soberly with his tragedies" is given a place among the most famous classical writers; and there is an interesting reference to the *Octavia* in More's *Utopia* (1516). Ascham indeed in *The Scholemaster* says: "Sophocles and Euripides far ouermatch our *Seneca* in Latin, namely in οἰκονομία et *Decoro*, although *Senacaes* elocution and verse be verie commend-

---

[1] See R. Peiper *Chaucer und seine Vorbilder im Alterthum* in *Jahrbb. für Class. Philologie* (1868) p. 65. Even before Chaucer's time, Nicholas Trevet or Trivet, an English Dominican friar, shared with Alberto Mussato the honour of reviving the study of Seneca. A specimen of his annotations on the tragedies is given in the preface to the edition of his *Annales* published by the English Historical Society, and the complete manuscript is in the British Museum. We might go further back still and establish a connection between Seneca and the Anglo-Saxon, Aldhelm.

able for his tyme;" but the way in which he speaks of
"our Seneca" seems to imply that the Roman dramatist
was far more familiar to his readers. Ascham, unlike most
of his contemporaries, was "a verie good Grecian"—a debt
he owed to the teaching of Sir John Cheke, whose dictum
he quotes with approval that a good student should
"dwell" in Cicero only of the Latin writers; the rest he
should "passe and iorney through." Ascham himself
boldly asserts the superiority of Greek authors to those of
all other nations, ancient or modern. "Cicero onelie
excepted, and one or two moe in Latin, they be all
patched cloutes and ragges, in comparison of faire wouen
broade cloathes. And trewelie, if there be any good in
them, it is either lerned, borowed, or stolne, from some
one of those worthie wittes of *Athens.*" But it would be
a mistake to suppose that this was an opinion generally
held; we shall get much nearer to the ordinary standard
of scholarship and the popular view of classical literature

Webbe. in William Webbe, a Cambridge graduate and literary
critic, connected with our early drama by an introductory
letter he supplied to the revised edition of *Tancred and
Gismund* (1592). In his *Discourse of English Poetrie*
(1586), Webbe confesses that the poets he is best acquain-
ted with are "not all nor the moste part of the auncient
Grecians, of whom I know not how many there were, but
these of the Latinists, which are of the greatest fame
and most obuious among vs." He thinks Virgil at least
equal to Homer, and asks of the Roman poets generally
in Virgil's time, "Wherein were they not comparable
with the Greekes?" In his review of the Latin poets he

makes mention of Seneca, "a most excellent wryter of Tragedies;" and in his list of translators he has a graceful reference to "the laudable Authors of *Seneca* in English." Even Ascham, in another passage of *The Scholemaster*, gives Seneca a place alongside of Euripides and Sophocles as models of tragedy—an example followed by Puttenham in his *Arte of English Poesie* (1589). To Sidney, to Meres, and to Shakspere[1] himself, Seneca was the model of classical tragedy; and it was "the famous Corduban" that the ambitious tragedians of Hall's *Satires* (1597) strove to excel. There is every indication that the knowledge of Greek tragedy was confined to a very small circle; translations from the Greek dramatists were unknown in this century, Gascoigne's *Jocasta* being, as has already been remarked, an Italian adaptation. The first genuine translation of a Greek play was apparently the *Electra* of Christopher Wase, printed at the Hague in 1649; and it was not until more than a century later that there appeared the first complete translation of a Greek tragic poet—Francklin's *Sophocles* (1759). All the evidence is in favour of Dr. Campbell's statement that "English students of the drama contented themselves with Seneca."[2] The translation of 1581 was ready to hand, and in 1623-4 Thomas Farnabie published an edition of the original with notes,[3] which must have been exceedingly useful. Seneca was a

---

[1] Sidney praises *Gorboduc* as "clyming to the height of Seneca his style," Shakspere is compared by Meres to Seneca, and Polonius says of the players in *Hamlet*, "Seneca cannot be too heavy, nor Plautus too light" for them.
[2] *A Guide to Greek Tragedy*, p. 309.
[3] Of this issue twenty editions were published. Munro.

Seneca read at School. favourite school author, and Professor T. S. Baynes has come to the conclusion that Shakspere read the tragedies at Stratford Grammar School.¹ The afternoon lessons of the boys at Rotherham School in Shakspere's time were "two days in Horace, and two days in Seneca's Tragedies; both which they translated into English." Hoole, one of the masters at Rotherham School, setting forth a model curriculum in his *New Discovery*, published in 1659, but written 23 years before, and well-known previous to publication, says, "As for Lucan, Seneca's Tragedies, Martial, and the rest of the finest Latin poets, you may do well to give them a taste of each, and show them how and wherein they may *Imitated and borrowed from.* imitate them, and borrow something out of them." This "imitation" and "borrowing" was a lesson well learnt by the dramatists, as I shall have occasion to show hereafter. Enough has already been said to show the esteem in which Seneca was held by the Elizabethans, and if his connection with the drama be deemed to be as yet insufficiently established, proof may easily be found in the Latin quotations from Seneca embodied in the text of many Elizabethan tragedies.² The fact of Seneca's influence upon the English drama being thus proved, we may proceed to examine the general character of this influence before we inquire into its exact extent.

---

[1] See *What Shakespeare learnt at School* in *Fraser's Magazine* for November, 1879.
[2] See Appendix I.

In any attempt to estimate the position of Seneca *Senecan Controversies.* in the developement of the modern drama, we are met at the outset by controversies which offer inviting fields for discussion. Who was the Seneca to whom the tragedies are ascribed? How many of them are genuinely his? Who wrote those that are wrongly ascribed to him? Were the tragedies intended for representation on the stage, or are they to be regarded as mere rhetorical exercises, meant only for private recitation? These are questions which have agitated the minds of critics and scholars for nearly three hundred years, but it would be a mistake to pay attention to them when treating Seneca from the point of view of the Elizabethan drama. The authors of the translation of 1581 were troubled by no critical doubts or difficulties; they had no idea that the very title of their volume, "Seneca his Tenne Tragedies," was open to objection. In his dedicatory letter Newton unhesitatingly identifies the author of the tragedies with Seneca the philosopher; he is evidently entirely ignorant of any suggestion that the *Thebais* is simply a patchwork of two fragments; and he and his fellow translators are equally blind to the fact that the *Octavia* for chronological reasons, and the *Hercules Oetaeus* for critical reasons cannot be accepted as the work of Seneca. Nevyle takes it for granted that the *Oedipus* was originally intended for "tragicall and Pompous showe upon Stage," and the confidence with which Jasper Heywood dubs Seneca "the flowre of all writers" is almost amusing in view of the depth of disrepute to which the tragedies have fallen since. I have thought it best in this

The Elizabethan point of view. essay to take the tragedies as far as possible from the Elizabethan point of view. From this point of view it is correct to speak of the author of the tragedies simply as Seneca, without any cumbrous qualifications; and I shall call the tragedies by the names given to them by the Elizabethans, though no doubt it would be more correct to treat the *Thebais* as made up of a fragmentary *Oedipus* and a fragmentary *Phoenissae*. The text quoted is the Aldine of Avantius (1517), which has been the foundation of most subsequent editions. Peiper and Richter say in their preface, " Si universum spectamus, nullum librum uel manu scriptum uel inpressum fatendum est tam prope ad genuinam recensionis uolgaris condicionem accedere quam Aldinam." As I was not in a position to see a copy of the Aldine edition, I have restored the readings of Avantius in the text of Peiper and Richter published in 1867, and the figures refer to the numbering of the lines in that edition.

Seneca is
1. Modern,   It would be easy to convict Seneca of many and very serious shortcomings; it would not be difficult to prove that by the side of obvious defects he possesses some excellences. Klein praises the scene between Andromache and Ulysses in the *Troas* as unsurpassed even by Shakspere; and Dryden says of the same passage that it "bears the nearest resemblance of anything in the tragedies of the ancients to the excellent scenes of passion in Shakespeare or in Fletcher." Leaving aside all question of intrinsic merit, this is the first quality I wish to claim for Seneca

—that he is the most modern of the ancients; in the words of Klein, he "stands nearer to Shakspeare and Calderón than to Euripides." Even if Greek tragedy had stood within as easy reach of the Elizabethans as Seneca, it may be doubted whether they would have been able to assimilate it; its perfectness would not make it any easier to imitate, and it was as far removed from modern ideas in spirit as in form. The whole of Greek tragedy is thoroughly Athenian in spirit, its conceptions are all of the ancient Greek world, and its form, its very conventions were vitally affected by the circumstances that had given it birth and assisted in its developement. Seneca is nearer to the moderns in spirit than in time. In his case the local conditions which moulded Greek tragedy were absent. His stoicism, his personal circumstances, and the spirit of his time all helped to make him cosmopolitan. "The age of Nero" (I quote from my notes of a lecture by Dr. Ward) "may be regarded as the climax of a cosmopolitan tendency in literature, which began under the Republic itself, and was no longer satisfied with what appealed only to Roman sentiment. There was no national life at Rome in the time of Nero, hardly a national literature, no national drama." Seneca is peculiarly free from local restrictions, and to this we may perhaps ascribe the fact that Elizabethan tragedy, though thrilled through and through with patriotism, deals with men and ideas of universal interest. Shakspere glorified some of his plays with an impassioned spirit of healthy patriotism, but of his masterpieces it is peculiarly true that they are "not of an age, but for all time."

3. *Introspective.* In another way Seneca stands nearer to the modern drama than to Greek tragedy. "Ancient tragedy" says Dr. Campbell [1] "is stamped with a degree of objectivity and outwardness which, on the whole, differentiates its creations from those of the modern drama, steeped as this so often is with the introspectiveness or self-reflectiveness that pervades the modern world." We note the beginning of the change in Euripides; but in Seneca it is very plainly marked. The scene is no longer in the open air, but within doors. The plots of Atreus and their bloody execution, the guilty suit of Phaedra, and the machinations of Deianira and Medea could not take place before a temple or in the courtyard of a palace. Seneca's arrangement of the plot in all these cases implies secresy and concealment; and introspectiveness follows as a matter of course upon his mode of treatment. Sir Walter Scott says in his preface to Dryden's *Oedipus*: "Though devoid of dramatic effect, of fancy, and of genius, the *Oedipus* of Seneca displays the masculine eloquence and high moral sentiment of its author; and if it does not interest us in the scene of fiction, it often compels us to turn our thoughts inward, and to study our own hearts." The remark is equally true of the other plays. In the *Thyestes* Atreus is introduced brooding over his own supineness in not seeking revenge; and when Thyestes enters, he is lost in reflection on the subject of his own doubts and fears. Oedipus and Jocasta in the *Thebais* are the subjects of the same morbid self-analysis. The thoughts of Phaedra in love,

---
[1] *A Guide to Greek Tragedy*, p. 38.

of Medea in hatred, of Deianira in jealousy revolve round one centre—themselves. In the *Agamemnon* Clytemnestra shows the same tendency to soliloquy and self-examination, her first words being

> quid segnis animë tuta consilia expetis ?
> quid fluctuaris ?

We shall find nothing in Greek tragedy so near as this to the scruples of Macbeth and the self-analysis of Hamlet.

Seneca's introspectiveness is chiefly due to the character of his themes and his mode of dealing with them. The sensationalism which Aristotle and Aristophanes remark in Euripides is still more marked in Seneca. His subjects are indeed taken from Greek tragedy, but they are the most sensational he could choose—the horrid banquet of Thyestes, the murder of Agamemnon by his faithless wife and her paramour, the guilty love of Phaedra, the execution of Astyanax and Polyxena, the revenge of Medea, the slaughter of Megára and her children, the fatal jealousy of Deianira, the incest and parricide of Oedipus and the unnatural strife of his sons. In the *Octavia*, the only tragedy whose subject is not taken from Greek mythology, the theme is still of lust and blood. Perhaps the example of Seneca was hardly needed to direct Elizabethan tragedy into the same channel. Those were stirring and licentious times, and the nation which kept Spain and the Inquisition at bay abroad had memories at home of the lustfulness of

Henry, the cruelty of Mary, and the intrigues of Elizabeth. The moral atmosphere of the court did not improve in the following reign, and it was no wonder that English dramatists continued to treat of lawless love and prodigious crimes; by this time the example of Seneca had been re-inforced by the influence of the Italian and the Spanish drama, in which the same leaven had been at work.

5. Rhetorical. Seneca goes to no trouble to make his sensational themes dramatically effective by clever construction of plot and careful developement of character. He contents himself with amplifying the horror of the tragic situations till they become disgusting, and exaggerating the expression of passion till it becomes ridiculous. In *Hercules Furens* 1291-1301 we have an example of the style to which Nick Bottom gave the immortal title of " Ercles' vein "[1]:—

> arma nisi dentur mihi,
> aut omne Pindi thracis excidam nemus
> Bacchique lucos et Cithaeronis iuga
> mecum cremabo. tota cum domibus suis
> dominisque tecta, cum deis templa omnibus
> thebana supra corpus excipiam meum
> atque urbe uersa condar et si fortibus
> leue pondus umeris moenia inmissa excident
> septemque opertus non satis portis premar,
> onus omne media parte qua mundus sedet
> dirimitque superos in meum uertam caput.

---

[1] In *Lingua*, a play acted at one of the Universities in the reign of Elizabeth, Tactus "cannot be otherwise persuaded but he is *Hercules Furens*," and beats Appetitus, who sets himself to "outswagger him."

This rhetorical exaggeration is best known to us in the school of English tragedy headed by *Tamburlaine*; but we shall find that in the later Elizabethans it is not absent. Shakspere uses it not infrequently, but always in a white heat of passion that goes far towards making hyperbole pardonable. There is a notable example in the grave scene in *Hamlet* (V. 1 *ad fin.*); and Munro[1] compares *Thyestes* 289-292:—

> regna nunc sperat mea.
> hac spe minanti fulmen occurret Iovi,
> hac spe subibit gurgitis tumidi minas
> dubiumque libycae Syrtis intrabit fretum,

with the words of Hotspur in 1 *Henry IV*, I. 3:—

> By heaven, methinks it were an easy leap,
> To pluck bright honour from the pale-faced moon,
> Or dive into the bottom of the deep.........

We have other examples in the speech of Juliet, IV. 1:—

> O, bid me leap, rather than marry Paris,
> From off the battlements of yonder tower.........

and in *The Merchant of Venice*, IV. 1:—

> You may as well go stand upon the beach,
> And bid the main flood bate his usual height.........

Seneca was much given to these exaggerated comparisons. See *Hercules Furens* 376-382; *Thyestes* 476-482; *Hippolytus* 576-581; *Octavia* 227-231; *Hercules Oetaeus* 338-341 and 1586-1590.

---

[1] *Journal of Philology*, VI. 77.

6. Descriptive. Without regular dramatic development by action and character, the tragedies of Seneca are filled up with elaborate descriptions, sententious dialogues, and reflective diatribes. Of Seneca's descriptive passages little need be said; they are the forerunners of similar efforts by the Elizabethan dramatists, who excel Seneca as much in descriptive power as they show moderation in the use of it; particular resemblances will be pointed out hereafter. So far as space goes, narrative plays a great part in Seneca's tragedies; but much of it is mere padding;

7. Reflective. far more characteristic of Seneca are the reflective passages, and the dialogue, which is highly finished in form and often heavily weighted with philosophic thought.

Stichomythia. Stichomythia is very common in Seneca's tragedies, and sometimes every line is a moral maxim or a commonplace of philosophy. English playwrights very soon began to imitate Seneca's brilliant performances in this respect, and it is interesting to mark the steps of their progress. *Gorboduc* (1561) yields us no example, but we have already an attempt, though not a very successful one, in *Damon and Pythias* (printed in 1571, and probably acted and published a few years before; it was licensed in 1567) e.g. Hazlitt's Dodsley, IV. p. 56:—

> DION. Take heed for [your] life: wordly men break promise in many things.
> PITH. Though wordly men do so, it never haps amongst friends.
> DION. What callest thou friends? are they not men, is not this true?
> PITH. Men they be, but such men as love one another only for virtue.
> DION. For what virtue dost thou love this spy, this Damon?
> PITH. For that virtue which yet to you is unknown.

The Misfortunes of Arthur (1587-8) and the revised version of *Tancred and Gismund* (pub. 1592) show a considerable advance, both in quality and quantity, many of the lines being borrowed directly from Seneca. In *The Spanish Tragedy* we have fairly finished stichomythia with greater originality. Marlowe's dialogue is not particularly striking, but Peele's *Edward I* gives us a remarkable example. Mr. Bullen's edition, Scene XXI.:—

> LONGSH. Why what remains for Baliol now to give?
> BALIOL. Allegiance, as becomes a royal king.
> LONGSH. What league of faith where league is broken once?
> BALIOL. The greater hope in them that once have fall'n.
> LONGSH. But foolish are those monarchs that do yield
>   A conquered realm upon submissive vows.

Shakspere has many such passages,[1] of which it will be enough to quote one, and that a short one. *The Merchant of Venice*, IV. 1 :—

> BASS. This no answer, thou unfeeling man,
>   To excuse the current of thy cruelty.
> SHY. I am not bound to please thee with my answer.
> BASS. Do all men kill the things they do not love?
> SHY. Hates any man the thing he would not kill?
> BASS. Every offence is not a hate at first.
> SHY. What, wouldst thou have a serpent sting thee twice?

Seneca is not content with elaborating brilliant dialogue in alternate lines; he balances half, third, and quarter lines. Thus in the *Medea*, 168-173 :—

---

[1] See *Richard III, passim*, especially IV. 4; 1 *Henry VI*, IV. 5; and 3 *Henry VI*, III. 2.

```
Nvtr.   rex est timendus.
Med.                        rex meus fuerat pater.
Nvtr.   non metuis arma?
Med.                        sint licet terra edita.
Nvtr.   moriere.
Med.            cupio.
Nvtr.                   profuge.
Med.                            paenituit fugae.
        Medea fugiam?
Nvtr.                   mater es.
Med.                            cui sim uides.
Nvtr.   profugere dubitas?
Med.                            fugiam, at ulciscar prius.
Nvtr.   uindex sequetur.
Med.                            forsan inueniam moras.
```

Hughes makes obvious efforts to imitate this trick of style in *The Misfortunes of Arthur*. (See Hazlitt's Dodsley, IV. 268, 277, 283, 284, 286, 303.) We have less elaborate but more successful attempts in *Tancred and Gismund* (Hazlitt's Dodsley, VII. 70, 73, 88, 92.) In the opening scenes of *Hamlet* Shakspere has used a like brevity with a very different effect. The appearance of artificiality is removed by occasional irregularity, which has the semblance of carelessness, but is really the outcome of the highest art; and to the majesty of verse is added the naturalness of ordinary conversation.

Seneca's Philosophy. Seneca's reflective passages are by no means confined to dialogue. Long speeches give him opportunity for rhetorical expansion, and the Chorus occasionally developes a philosophic theme. For the most part the subjects of reflection are familiar commonplaces—the cares of empire, the fickleness of fortune, the uncertainty of popular favour, the cruelty of war, the falsehood of fame, the impetuosity of youth, the modesty of maidenhood, the evil consequences of luxury, the fatal gift of beauty, the dangers of high places and the safety of humility, the joys of a country life and the advantages of poverty. Similar reflections are frequent in the Elizabethan dramatists, and I shall point out many instances in which Seneca's form of expression is reproduced with more or less exactness. Shakspere deals freely in this small coin of philosophy, but he generally issues it new *Aphorisms.* from his own mint. A line in *Cymbeline*, IV.3:—

> Some falls are means the happier to arise

suggests a comparison with *Troas* 896-7:—

> hic forsitan te casus excelso magis
> solio reponet.

But this may be merely a coincidence; and the same remark applies to most Shaksperean parallels with Seneca, as we shall see later on. So in *Julius Caesar*, I.3:—

> Nor stony tower, nor walls of beaten brass,
> Nor airless dungeon, nor strong links of iron,
> Can be retentive to the strength of spirit;
> But life, being weary of these worldly bars,
> Never lacks power to dismiss itself.

Thebais 151-3:—

> ubique mors est. optume hoc cauit deus.
> eripere uitam nemo non homini potest,
> at nemo mortem; mille ad hanc aditus patent.

We have an unacknowledged translation in *The Misfortunes of Arthur*, I. 3:—

> Each-where is death! the fates have well ordain'd,
> That each man may bereave himself of life,
> But none of death: death is so sure a doom,
> A thousand ways do guide us to our graves.

Marston also keeps closer to Seneca's form. 1 *Antonio and Mellida*, III. 2:—

> Each man take[s] hence life, but no man death:
> He's a good fellow, and keeps open house:
> A thousand thousand ways lead to his gate,
> To his wide-mouthed porch, when niggard life
> Hath but one little, little wicket through.

Beaumont and Fletcher tell us that to death "a thousand doors are open." Massinger says in *The Duke of Milan*, I. 3:—

> There are so many ways to let out life.

and Shirley, in *Love's Cruelty*, V. 1:—

> A thousand ways there are to let out life.

It is curious how some of Seneca's aphorisms do duty again and again in the Elizabethan drama with but slight changes of form. Seneca had written in the *Agamemnon*:—

> per scelera semper sceleribus tutum est iter.

This is translated by Studley:—

> The safest path to mischiefe is by mischiefe open still.

Thomas Hughes has it in *The Misfortunes of Arthur*,
I. 4:—
    The safest passage is from bad to worse.

Marston in *The Malcontent*, V. 2:—
    Black deed only through black deed safely flies.

Shakspere in *Macbeth*, III. 2:—
    Things bad begun make strong themselves by ill.

Jonson in *Catiline*, I. 2:—
    The ills that I have done cannot be safe
    But by attempting greater.

Webster in *The White Devil*, II. 1:—
    Small mischiefs are by greater made secure.

Lastly, in Massinger's *Duke of Milan*, II. 1 Francisco says
    All my plots
    Turn back upon myself; but I am in,
    And must go on: and, since I have put off
    From the shore of innocence, guilt be now my pilot!
    Revenge first wrought me; murder's his twin brother:
    One deadly sin, then, help to cure another!

In addition to a large stock of brilliant commonplaces, there is in the tragedies a considerable body of thought which is part of Seneca's philosophic faith. The leading doctrine is that of fatalism—not the fatalism *Fatalism.* of Aeschylus, which is one with the will of the gods, and makes for righteousness,[1] but the absolute, hopeless

---

[1] See *Supplices* (Paley) 1031-4 and *Prometheus* 526-7; also an article on "Aeschylus as a Religious Teacher" in the *Contemporary Review* for 1866, by Mr. (now Bishop) Brooke Foss Westcott, republished in his recent *Essays in the History of Religious Thought in the West*.

fatalism of the Stoic school, which includes the gods themselves in its universal sway.

> omnia certo tramite uadunt
> primusque dies dedit extremum.
> non illa deo uertisse licet
> quae nexa suis currunt causis. (*Oedipus* 1008-1011.)

As Nisard points out,[1] the fatalism of Greek tragedy is religious; that of Seneca is philosophic. In spite of his frequent use of the traditional mythology, Seneca is inclined to be sceptical. On returning to his native land, Thyestes addresses his ancestral gods with the doubtful addition, "si sunt tamen di." In spite of the ghosts in the *Troas*, the Chorus treat existence after death as an open question, and finally come to the conclusion

> Taenara et aspero
> regnum sub domino limen et obsidens
> custos non facili Cerberus ostio
> rumores uacui uerbaque inania
> et par sollicito fabula somnio.   (413-17.)

Even where Seneca accepts the traditional mythology, he attributes to the gods that envy of human pre-eminence which Aeschylus disowned.[2] Seneca has no faith in the righteous government of the world. The Chorus in the *Hippolytus* sing

> res humanas ordine nullo
> fortuna regit, spargitque manu
> munera caeca, peiora fouens.
> uincit sanctos dira libido,
> fraus sublimi regnat in aula.   (986-90.)

---

[1] In *Etudes sur les Poëtes Latins de la Décadence.*
[2] Cf. *Hippolytus* 1132-1152 with Aeschylus *Agamemnon* 727-737.

Mr. Swinburne, in an article on Webster in the *Nineteenth Century* for June, 1886, says, "Aeschylus is above all things the poet of righteousness. 'But in any wise, I say unto thee, revere thou the altar of righteousness:' this is the crowning admonition of his doctrine, as its crowning prospect is the reconciliation or atonement of the principle of retribution with the principle of redemption, of the powers of the mystery of darkness with the co-eternal forces of the spirit of wisdom, of the lord of inspiration and of light. The doctrine of Shakespeare, where it is not vaguer, is darker in its implication of injustice, in its acceptance of accident, than the impression of the doctrine of Aeschylus. Fate, irreversible and inscrutable, is the only force of which we feel the impact, of which we trace the sign, in the upshot of *Othello* or *King Lear*. The last step into the darkness remained to be taken by 'the most tragic' of all English poets. With Shakespeare—and assuredly not with Aeschylus—righteousness itself seems subject and subordinate to the masterdom of fate: but fate itself, in the tragic world of Webster, seems merely the servant or the synonym of chance." Seneca's fatalism is not peculiar to Webster, though he perhaps carried it further than any of his contemporaries. Fatalism of a more or less pronounced character runs through Elizabethan tragedy from the very beginning. When Heywood added to the *Troas* (pub. 1559) a Chorus of his own composition, though moulded on Seneca's style, this was one of the doctrines he chose for presentation. Folio 101 :—

> They sit aboue, that holde our life in line,
> And what we suffer downe they fling from hie,

> No carke, no care, that euer may vntwine
> The thrids, that wouen are aboue the skie.

We have the same note struck in *Gorbuduc* and *The Misfortunes of Arthur*, the latter simply translating the lines from the *Oedipus* quoted above:—

> All things are rul'd in constant course : no fate
> But is foreset : the first day leads the last.

In *Tancred and Gismund* we have :—

> His doom of death was dated by his stars,
> And who is he that may withstand his fate ?

As to Shakspere and the later Elizabethans, abundant evidence will be given hereafter.

Stoicism.

With Seneca's fatalism is closely connected his Stoical indifference to the accidents of life. *Thyestes* 615-18 :—

> nemo confidat nimium secundis,
> nemo desperet meliora lapsis :
> miscet haec illis prohibetque Clotho
> stare fortunam, rotat omne fatum.

In its full extent Seneca's Stoicism went further than this, and taught absolute independence of circumstances. This is effectively expressed by Medea, when, hopeless and friendless in a hostile land, she defies despair, exclaiming, "Medea superest"

> **fortuna opes auferre non animum potest.**

Amphitryon expresses the same idea in *Hercules Furens* 468:—

> quemcumque fortem uideris, miserum neges.

A full exposition of Stoical teaching on this point is given by the Chorus in the *Thyestes* (344-403), from which I will quote one short extract—

> rex est qui metuet nihil
> rex est qui cupiet nihil.
> meus regnum bona possidet
> hoc regnum sibi quisque dat.[1]

Along with this indifference to the accidents of life comes contempt for the final accident of death, as we note in the same Chorus:— *Contempt for Death.*

> rex est qui posuit metus
> et diri mala pectoris,
> ... ...
> qui tuto positus loco
> infra se uidet omnia
> occurritque suo libens
> fato nec queritur mori.

The spirit of the last lines is breathed by all Seneca's characters; all show the same invincible resolution in face of death. Phaedra, Deianira, and Jocasta fall by their own hands; Astyanax and Polyxena meet death not only bravely, but eagerly; Octavia, Cassandra, Electra, and Antigone show the same masculine constancy; death

---

[1] This is Peiper and Richter's reading, their arrangement of the lines being preferable to that of the Aldine text.

is the refuge desired by Oedipus and Hercules in shame, by Theseus and Thyestes in calamity; even Jason and Aegisthus, in all else cowards confessed, show a readiness for death equal to that of the bravest and best. We find this contempt for death again and again in the Elizabethan drama, and in the villains as well as in the heroes. We find it, too, often associated, as in Seneca, with fatalism. Thus Young Mortimer in Marlowe's *Edward II*, V. 6, when sentence of death is pronounced upon him for treason, adultery, and murder, says:—

> Base Fortune, now I see, that in thy wheel
> There is a point, to which when men aspire,
> They tumble headlong down: that point I touched,
> And, seeing there was no place to mount up higher,
> Why should I grieve at my declining fall?—
> Farewell, fair queen; weep not for Mortimer,
> That scorns the world, and, as a traveller,
> Goes to discover countries yet unknown.

Shakspere's villains—Richard III, Macbeth, and Gloster's bastard son—die with desperate fortitude, and Iago receives his condemnation in sullen silence. The Stoical fortitude of the heroines of Elizabethan tragedy is equally remarkable. For the present let one instance suffice. *The Winter's Tale*, III. 2:—

> LEON. Look for no less than death.
> HER.   Sir, spare your threats:
> The bug which you would fright me with I seek.
> To me can life be no commodity.

Compare *Troas* 583-6:—

ANDR. tuta est perire quae potest debet cupit.
VL. magnifica uerba mors prope admota excutit.
ANDR. si uis Vlixe cogere Andromacham metu,
uitam minare : nam mori uotum est mihi.

Seneca's women are on a level with his men in cour- *Seneca's Women*
age, in strength of will and mental power, whether in
arguing or planning, in initiation or in execution. But
perhaps it would be going too far to claim for Seneca
that he helped to bring about the different position
held by woman in the Romantic drama to that she
occupied in Greek tragedy; the advance is not merely
a literary phenomenon; it is a change in the spirit
and customs of the age. The same is to be said of
Klein's remark that upon the *Phaedra* Seneca may
ground a claim to have created the modern tragedy *Love-tragedy.*
of love, though the suggestion is not without plausibility.
Nisard says that the love of Phaedra is sensual love, that
of a prostitute; to which it may be replied that no
presentation of Phaedra's guilty passion would make it
pure or even worthy of sympathy. Euripides overcame
the difficulty by representing her passion as a divine
visitation beyond her own control; Seneca makes little
of this, and reduces love to its merely human elements.
Here, again, Seneca comes nearer to the moderns, by
disregarding that very element of fate, which in another
way brings him into close connection with them. Though
he propounds philosophic fatalism in Chorus and dialogue,
Seneca makes little of it in his delineation of character.
His personages may utter fatalistic apothegms, and be at
times the victims of circumstances; but in moral action

Conscience-tragedy. they give every evidence of free-will. The repentance of Thyestes, the remorse of Hercules and of Deianira, the hesitation of Medea, the uncertainty of Clytemnestra, the anxiety of Poppaea, and the increased moral sensitiveness of Agamemnon—all point to what Klein describes as "die Uebergangsstellung der römischen Tragödie zwischen der Schicksalidee der Griechen und der Gewissenstragik des von der christlichen Bussstimmung angeregten und von Shakspeare abgeschlossenen Sühnespiels." But all these are ingenious theories supported by very slight evidence; we must return to the solid ground of fact.

External form. The most obvious way in which Seneca affected the modern drama was in external form. From Seneca the European drama in general, and English tragedy in particular, received the five acts which have become the rule of the modern stage. In the Greek drama the number of ἐπεισόδια was variable; the division into five acts was apparently established by Varro, and is noted by Horace in the *Ars Poetica* as a rule to be strictly observed;[1] but it was the example of Seneca that governed the practice of the modern stage. Seneca's division into five acts separated by choruses is exactly reproduced in our earliest tragedies—in *Gorboduc*, in *The Misfortunes of Arthur*, and in *Tancred and Gismund*. The *The Chorus.* usage of Seneca with respect to the Chorus is retained in Gascoigne's *Jocasta*, in Kyd's *Cornelia*, in the Countess

---

[1] See Prof. Wilkins' note (line 189), and O. Ribbeck *Römische Tragödie*, p. 642.

of Pembroke's *Antony*, in Daniel's *Cleopatra* and *Philotas*, in Jonson's *Catiline*, in Lord Brooke's *Alaham* and *Mustapha*, and in Stirling's *Monarchicke Tragedies;* but it was a device foreign to the dramatic genius of the English people, and did not long keep its place on the popular stage in its original form and purpose. In *The Spanish Tragedy* Andrea and Revenge

> sit down to see the mystery
> And serve for Chorus in this Tragedy.

In *Soliman and Perseda* the same office is performed by Love, Fortune, and Death. There are three choruses in *Faustus*, two (three acts) in Peele's *David and Bethsabe*, one in *Romeo and Juliet*. Shakspere's use of the Chorus in *Henry V* is very different to the manner of Seneca; whose choruses could be cut out without any injury to the plot, and in some cases might even be transferred from one tragedy to another without any loss of appropriateness. Indeed the choruses of Seneca have often no more relation to the conduct of the plot than the lyrics with which the Eliztbethans adorned their plays. In *Henry V* the Chorus becomes a necessary part of the action, and at the same time gives the dramatist the opportunity of calling upon the spectators to eke out the historic and scenic illusion by the aid of imagination :—

Shakspere's Chorus.

> Think, when we talk of horses, that you see them
> Printing their proud hoofs i' the receiving earth ;
> For 'tis your thoughts that now must deck our kings,
> Carry them here and there ; jumping o'er times,
> Turning the accomplishment of many years
> Into an hour-glass : for the which supply,
> Admit me Chorus to this history.

This Shaksperean usage is a notable advance on classical authority, and was peculiar to the Elizabethan stage. The Chorus was used in this way at a later date by Fletcher and Massinger in *The Prophetess*; and Thomas Heywood by this means eked out the imperfect action of *If you know not me, you know no Bodie, or The Troubles of Queen Elizabith*.[1] Raynulph Higden in Middleton's *Mayor of Queenborough*, and Gower in *Pericles* are also much less satisfactory figures than the Chorus in *Henry V* with its soul-stirring patriotism and magnificent verse; and while we cannot but be thankful for a form of art of which we have immortal examples like the choruses of *Henry V*, on the whole we can hardly regret that the Chorus took the path

Disappearance of the Chorus. marked out for it by the developement of the drama, and disappeared from the modern stage. Seneca's use of the Chorus was a plain forewarning of its ultimate fate. In the early plays of Aeschylus supreme importance is attached to the Chorus, which was the kernel from which the drama had sprung. In Sophocles the Chorus has become subordinate to the dialogue. In Euripides its connection with the action is often slight; in Seneca this connection disappears altogether; the Chorus is already on its way to exclusion from the play and final disuse.

The Chorus on the Roman Stage. Agathon had introduced independent ἐμβόλιμα into Greek tragedy; but the important step was taken when the Chorus was excluded from the orchestra in the Roman

---

[1] The Chorus is first found in the edition of 1632; it is not in the editions of 1605-6.

theatre, and given a place on the stage. When this change was once effected, the presence of the Chorus was no longer necessary to the conduct of the action. An examination of the fragments of early Roman tragedy shows that the Chorus sometimes stayed on the stage throughout the action, sometimes went on and off according to the exigencies of the plot.¹ Seneca's Chorus seems to have been invariably absent during the progress of the action. He completely set at defiance the admonition of Horace:—

> actoris partis chorus officiumque uirile
> defendat, neu quid medios intercinat actus
> quod non proposito conducat et haereat apte.

The wording of *Hercules Furens* 831,

> densa sed laeto uenit
> clamore turba frontibus laurum gerens
> magnique meritas Herculis laudes canit,

shows that the Chorus only came on the stage to fill the pauses between the acts; and it took no other part in the play. Even where, as in the *Thyestes*, the Chorus is one of the interlocutors, immediately after it is assumed to be ignorant of the dialogue that has just taken place; and to make the passage at all reasonable, we must suppose that where the Chorus takes part in the action, its office is performed by the Coryphaeus alone, and that the other members of the Chorus are not present. Thus it comes about that, in answer to the questions of the

---
¹ See article by Otto Jahn in *Hermes* II., p. 226.

Chorus (or the Coryphaeus) the Messenger describes the murder of the children of Thyestes, and expresses his horror at the deed, ending his speech with the words:—

> uerterit cursus licet
> sibi ipse Titan obuium ducens iter
> tenebrisque facinus obruat tetrum nouis
> nox missa ab ortu tempore alieno grauis:
> tamen uidendum est, tota patefient mala.

But immediately after the Chorus want to know the reason of the darkness, and come to the conclusion that it must be the end of the world. Another suggestion to overcome this difficulty is the division of the Chorus; and still another explanation of Seneca's apparent carelessness on this point is to be found in the theory that the tragedies were not intended to be acted, but to be read. But, seeing that Seneca, in the plays now regarded as genuine, has taken the trouble to observe the rule of the three actors, it seems rash to assume that he committed such a glaring absurdity in the management of the Chorus. However that may be, it is clear that the Chorus was not supposed to be on the stage during the progress of the action. This is proved by *Hippolytus* 607-9:—

> PHAE. commodes paulum precor
> secretus aures. si quis est abeat comes.
> HIPP. en locus ab omni liber arbitrio uacat.

even though 832-6 might lead us to an opposite conclusion, for this is one of the few passages in Seneca which seem to presume that the Chorus has some knowledge of the course of the action. But it would be ridiculous to suppose that Phaedra preferred her shameful suit before the faces of a band of Athenian citizens, and that they afterwards allowed Hippolytus to be falsely accused in their presence when they could give direct evidence of his innocence. Medea cannot have unfolded her deep-laid scheme of vengeance in the ears of an unfriendly band of Corinthians, and Atreus could not have revealed the trap he was laying for his brother to the Chorus which sang immediately after :—

> tandem regia nobilis
> antiqui genus Inachi,
> fratrum conposuit minas.

A similar conclusion may be drawn from *Troas* 369-379; in the *Agamemnon*, the *Hercules Oetaeus*, and the *Octavia* there are two choruses, and the same argument holds good.

The absence of the Chorus during the progress of the action lessened Seneca's hold on the so-called "unities" of time and place, which were not arbitrary rules of the Greek drama, but natural consequences of the continuous presence of the Chorus. It used to be the fashion to base the unities on the authority of the Greek tragic poets and of Aristotle, but more recent criticism has discovered that the unities of time and place are by no means regularly observed in Greek tragedy,

The "Unities"

and Seneca has been made responsible for the cumbrous system of artificialities which was foisted upon the French classical drama. As a matter of fact, Seneca has no more respect for the unities than the Greeks. Aeschylus was apparently ignorant of any necessity for continuity of action; and the observance of Sophocles and Euripides is not without exceptions. Seneca makes some effort to conform to the precept of Aristotle, but he is not bound by any hard and fast line. As Lessing has shown,[1] no reasonable assumption will bring the action of the *Thyestes* within the limits of a single day; and the *Thebais* has a change of scene, even apart from its fragmentary composition. The action of the *Octavia* extends over at least three days. In line 604 Nero says

of Time

quin destinamus proximam thalamis diem?

On the day after the marriage Poppaea recounts a dream she has had during the past night, an insurrection caused by the divorce of Octavia is crushed, and Octavia sent into exile. The action of the *Hercules Oetaeus* begins in Oechalia, then changes to Trachis, and ends on Mount Oeta; and there are journeys to and from Oechalia and Trachis, which must have taken several days. Probably the most obvious offences against the unities of time and place are to be found in the plays wrongly ascribed to Seneca; but I have already pointed out that, for the Elizabethans, this distinction did not exist. The first

and Place.

---

[1] Theatralische Bibliothek, Erstes Stück (Lachmann) S. 321-3.

English tragedy, *Gorboduc*, begins, as in Seneca,[1] by marking the fact that the action opens at daybreak:—

> The silent night that bringes the quiet pawse,
> From painefull trauailes of the wearie daie,
> Prolonges my carefull thoughtes, and makes me blame
> The slowe *Aurore* that so, for loue or shame,
> Doth longe delaye to shewe her blushing face;
> And nowe the daie renewes my griefull plainte.

These lines are quite in Seneca's style, and might almost be a patchwork from the openings of the *Octavia* and the *Oedipus*. But, as in the *Hercules Oetaeus*, no attempt is made to bring the action within the limits of a single day; armies are raised, and considerable journeys made in the course of the tragedy. The miracle plays had accustomed English audiences to absence of continuity, changes of scene, and a large number of actors, features which were exceptional or altogether lacking in ancient tragedy. The Elizabethans were probably not aware that Seneca observed the rule of three actors, for only a careful examination has revealed the fact that the genuine plays of Seneca are arranged for three actors, the pseudo-Senecan for four.

Three Actors.

Another maxim of the *Ars Poetica*, *Stage Decencies.*

> ne pueros coram populo Medea trucidet,

Seneca flagrantly violated. Medea kills both her children on the stage, and as she flies through the air in a winged

---

[1] See *Hercules Furens* 123-138; *Thyestes* 120-1; *Oedipus* 1-5; *Agamemnon* 53-6, *Octavia* 1-6.

car flings the bodies down at their father's feet. Phaedra and Jocasta stab themselves *coram populo*. In the *Thyestes* the precept of Horace is, from the necessities of the case, observed in the letter, but the Messenger's account of the sacrifice is drawn out in such sickening detail that the repellent effect is but slightly decreased; the same may be said of the death of Hippolytus. Commentators have generally assumed that Megara and her children are slain in view of the spectators, but Lessing and Pierrot contend that this is a mistake. Lessing's interpretation of the scene runs thus: "Hercules draws his bow and pierces one of his children with the arrow; the second, who clasps his father's knees with his little hands and begs for mercy in a piteous voice, is seized in that powerful grasp, swung round in the air, and dashed to pieces on the ground. While Hercules is pursuing the third, who flies for refuge to his mother, the latter is caught sight of, and taken for Juno. Hercules slays first his child, and then his wife.—All this, the reader will say, must make a very horrible and bloody spectacle. But in this place, by the help of the Roman stage, which was constructed on a very different plan to ours, the poet has introduced a very fine scene. As Hercules pursues his children and his wife, and from time to time goes out of sight of the spectators, all the murders take place behind the scenes, where they can only be seen by the other characters on the stage, above all by Amphitryon, who each moment describes all he sees, and thus informs the spectators of it in as lively a fashion as if they had seen it themselves." Heinsius is of opinion that the murders took place in view

of the spectators, and suggests that in this tragedy Nero
satisfied his lust for blood in the same way as in the case
of the Icarus who was dashed to pieces on the stage and
bespattered the tyrant with his gore. The text seems to
bear out the view of Lessing and Pierrot, but we may be
sure that the Elizabethans were unaware of this ingenious
explanation, which is by no means obvious to a critical
reader, much less to the unlearned.

Diversity of Practice.

The early Elizabethans show much diversity in their
observance of stage decencies. In *Gorboduc* and *The
Misfortunes of Arthur* the deaths are reported by a Messenger; but in contemporary tragedies intended for the
popular stage there is no such reserve. In *King Cambyses*
(c. 1561) Execution smites Sisamnes in the neck with a
sword "to signify his death," and "flays him with a
false skin" upon the command of the King, "Pull his
skin over his ears." Cruelty and Murder enter "with
bloody hands" to slay Smirdis, and after they have
stabbed him, "a little bladder of vinegar is pricked" to
represent his blood. In *Appius and Virginia* (pr. 1575,
acted 1563) we have the stage direction, "Here tie a
handkercher about her eyes, and then strike off her head;"
but there is no suggestion as to the means whereby this
feat was accomplished without injury to the actor of the
part; afterwards Virginius brings in Virginia's head—a
precedent in stage effect which had illustrious followers.
Appius and Virginia and *Cambyses* are both closely connected with the moralities, and it is probable that the

The Miracle Plays. practice of the miracle plays had considerable influence upon the English stage in this respect.¹ In the York, Chester, Coventry, and Towneley Mystery Plays the murder of Abel and the Crucifixion take place on the stage; in the Digby Mysteries the children of Bethlehem are slain on the stage, and Herod dies there. Though the authors of our first regular tragedies did not imitate the directness of the miracle plays in the action proper, they did not hesitate to represent deeds of violence and

The Dumb-Show murder on the stage in dumb-show. In *Gorboduc* and *The Misfortunes of Arthur* the dumb-show is allegorical; but in *Tancred and Gismund* it is sometimes realistic enough. Guiscard's death was represented thus:—"After Guiscard had kindly taken leave of them all, a strangling-cord was fastened about his neck, and he haled forth by them. Renuchio bewaileth it, and then, entering in, bringeth forth a standing cup of gold, with a bloody heart reeking hot in it, and then saith, *ut sequitur*." The speech that follows is moulded on that of the Messenger in the *Thyestes*. Gismunda dies

A Noteworthy Change. on the stage, but in this point there is a marked difference between the manuscript of 1568 and the revised edition of 1591. In the first version Gismunda is disposed of very quietly, the stage direction being merely "Gismonda

---

¹ To the influence of the miracle plays we should perhaps also ascribe the mixture of comedy and tragedy which is found in *Cambyses* and *Appius and Virginia*, and which afterwards became a distinctive mark of the romantic drama. Seneca has not the slightest hint of comedy, not even such an approach to it as the Watchman in the *Agamemnon* of Aeschylus and the *Antigone* of Sophocles, or the humours of Hercules in the *Alcestis* of Euripides.

dieth"; her father then makes a speech foreshadowing his own death, and goes off the stage; the epilogue informs us parenthetically that he "now himself hath slain." In the revised edition Gismunda's death scene is considerably enlarged, and Tancred puts out his eyes and kills himself on the stage. The change is a remarkable one, and is probably to be ascribed to the horrors of *The Spanish Tragedy* and the authority of Marlowe, which made it the rule of the English stage to follow the practice of Seneca. Sometimes the murders are presented on the stage, sometimes they are reported by the Messenger, a *The Messenger.* figure appearing with decreasing importance in Greek, Roman, and English tragedy. Shakespere represents all kinds of horrors *coram populo;* but he does not disdain the use of the traditional machinery, and sometimes his Messengers remind us of those of Seneca. Compare, for instance, *Romeo and Juliet*, V.1 :—

> O, pardon me for bringing these ill news,
> Since you did leave it for my office, sir.

with *Hippolytus* 1000-1 :—

> o sors acerba et dura famulatus grauis,
> cur me ad nefandos nuntium casus uocas ?

And *Macbeth*, IV. 3 :—

> Let not your ears despise my tongue for ever,
> Which shall possess them with the heaviest sound
> That ever yet they heard.

with *Troas* 533-5 :—

> durae minister sortis hoc primum peto,
> ut ore quamis uerba dicantur meo
> non esse credas nostra.

Other Stock Characters.

In addition to the Messenger, Seneca bestowed upon English tragedy other stock characters—the confidential Nurse, full of counsel and consolation; her male counterpart, the faithful Servant; and the cruel Tyrant, with his ambitious schemes and maxims of rule. But the most important inheritance of English tragedy in this respect was the Ghost. As Mr. J. A. Symonds says in *Shakspere's Predecessors,* "the Ghost, imported from Seneca into English tragedy, had a long and brilliant career." Much could be added to what Mr. Symonds has said on this point, but nothing could be said better. Attention may, however, be called to the important part played in Seneca's tragedies by supernatural agencies of all kinds. In the main, the use of the supernatural was a tradition received by Seneca from the Greeks; but he considerably enlarged the inheritance before he handed it on to English tragedy. If all the dramas of Aeschylus were extant, we might find that the author of the *Psychagogoi* equalled or surpass Seneca in this respect; but there is an appearance of probability in the suggestion of Dr. Campbell that in the *Eumenides* Aeschylus carried the staging of the supernatural too far for the temper of his age. Sophocles and Euripides rely less than Aechylus upon the use of the supernatural, and it was left for Seneca to develope the impressive effects of supernatural appearances and devices, and bequeath them to the modern stage. It is seldom the gods of the upper air whom he brings on the scene; the atmosphere he loves to breathe is that of the world below. In the *Hercules Furens* we have a full description of all the horrors of

The Ghost.

Use of the Supernatural.

Tartarus, and again and again in other plays the same
picture is drawn on a smaller canvas. Lethe, Cocytus,
Styx, Acheron, and Phlegethon are Seneca's best-loved
streams; Tantalus, Ixion, and Sisyphus his favourite
characters. The Ghost of Tantalus, driven by a Fury,
opens the *Thyestes*; the Ghost of Thyestes the *Agamemnon*; in the *Octavia* the Ghost of Agrippina appears. Laius
is called up from the shades in the *Oedipus*; the Ghosts
of Achilles and Hector are seen in visions in the *Troas*;
and we have another ghostly dream—that of Poppaea—in
the *Octavia*. Oedipus is terrified in the *Thebais* by the vision
of the murdered Laius, and Octavia's dreams are haunted
by the Ghost of Brittanicus. Atreus and Medea invoke the
Furies to aid them in their revenge; and when Medea is
relenting, she is spurred on by the appearance of her
murdered brother's spirit. It would take too long to
examine the various ways in which these suggestions of
Seneca were worked out by the Elizabethan dramatists;
a well-read student could easily call to mind a score of
parallels. I will only stay to draw attention to two less
obvious comparisons. Juliet is inspired with strength to
take the sleeping-potion by a like vision to that which
appeared to Medea in her moment of weakness:—

> O, look! methinks I see my cousin's ghost
> Seeking out Romeo, that did spit his body
> Upon a rapier's point: stay, Tybalt, stay!
> Romeo, I come! this do I drink to thee.[1]

---

[1] As to the form of the vision see also *Octavia* 123-7.

With the invocations of Medea and Atreus compare that of Lady Macbeth :—

> Come, you spirits
> That tend on mortal thoughts, unsex me here,
> And fill me, from the crown to the toe, top-full
> Of direst cruelty ! make thick my blood,
> Stop up the access and passage to remorse,
> That no compunctious visitings of nature
> Shake my fell purpose, nor keep peace between
> The effect and it ![1]

Besides ghosts and the Furies here invoked, two other supernatural devices used in *Macbeth* had been previously employed by Seneca—witchcraft and oracles. The latter we have in the *Oedipus* and the *Hercules Oetaeus*; the former in the *Hercules Oetaeus* and the *Medea*. Klein remarks that the ingredients contained in Medea's "Hexenkessel" vie in strange variety with the hotchpotch that Macbeth's witches throw into their caldron; and a passage in *The Tempest*, V. 1 (lines 41-50) may be compared with *Hercules Oetaeus* 457-466 and *Medea* 755-772.

A Contemporary Critic.

When we remember that sensational horrors presented on the stage, the Ghost, and the Chorus are among the most striking features of Seneca, it seems not a little remarkable that these very points should be selected by a contemporary critic as the most noteworthy characteristics of Elizabethan tragedy. In the Induction to *A Warning for*

---

[1] So *Thyestes* 249-254; *Medea* 13-17 and 973-4.

Faire Women (1599) we have the following description of contemporary tragedy :—

> How some damn'd tyrant to obtain a crown
> Stabs, hangs, impoisons, smothers, cutteth throats :
> And then a Chorus, too, comes howling in
> And tells us of the worrying of a cat:
> Then, too, a filthy whining ghost,
> Lapt in some foul sheet, or a leather pilch,
> Comes screaming like a pig half stick'd,
> And cries, Vindicta !—Revenge, Revenge !
> With that a little rosin flasheth forth,
> Like smoke out of a tobacco pipe, or a boy's squib.
> Then comes in two or three [more] like to drovers,
> With tailors' bodkins, stabbing one another—

The *Warning for Faire Women*, although it professess to be only a " true and home-born tragedy," is not altogether free from the faults criticised in the Induction. At the opening of Act II, Tragedy enters " with a bowl of blood in her hand," and speaks the following lines :—

> This deadly banquet is prepar'd at hand,
> Where Ebon tapers are brought up from hell
> To lead black Murther to this damned deed.
> The ugly Screech-owl and the night-Raven,
> With flaggy wings, and hideous croaking noise,
> Do beat the casements of this fatal house,
> Whilst I do bring my dreadful furies forth
> To spread the table to this bloody feast.

The height of sensational horror is finally reached in an execution on the stage.

Gorboduc

The authors of *Gorboduc*, the first English tragedy, as has been already pointed out, were guilty of no such offence against the decencies of the stage; and the connection of *Gorboduc* with Seneca as to external form and the observance of the unities has also been noticed.[1] Though we miss Seneca's brilliant dialogue, the resemblance in style is clear throughout. The long speeches and " grave sententious precepts " are unmistakeably in Seneca's manner,[2] and sometimes Seneca seems to be also responsible for the thought expressed. In Act II. 1 we have :—

> Knowe ye that lust of kingdomes hath no lawe ;
> The Goddes do beare and well allowe in kinges
> The thinges that they abhorre in rascall routes.
> When kinges on sclender quarrels ron to warres,
> And than in cruell and vnkindely wise,
> Commaunde theftes, rapes, murder of innocentes,
> To spoile of townes & reignes of mightie realmes,
> Thinke you such princes do suppose them selues
> Subiect to lawes of kinde and feare of Gods.
> Murders and violent theftes in priuate men
> Are heynous crymes and full of foule reproche,
> Yet none offence, but decked with glorious name
> Of noble conquestes in the handes of kinges.[3]

---

[1] See pp. 32, 39, 41.

[2] *Gorboduc* is praised by Sidney in the *Apologie for Poetrie* " as it is full of stately speeches, and well sounding Phrases, clyming to the height of Seneca his stile." Sidney's entire criticism of *Gorboduc* is interesting, but it is too long for quotation.

[3] The last four lines are differently arranged in the various editions, but this seems to be the right order. It is the reading of the 2nd edition (the first authorised edition), which is generally the best.

This passage appears to be an expansion of *Agamemnon* 265 and 270-3 :—

> lex alia solio est alia priuato toro.
> ....
> ignota tibi sunt iura regnorum haud noua.
> nobis maligni iudices aequi sibi
> id esse regni maximum pignus putant,
> si quicquid aliis non licet, solis licet.

Compare also V. 1 :—

> So giddie are the common peoples mindes,
> So glad of change, more wauerynge than the sea,

with the "fluctuque magis mobile uulgus" of *Hercules Furens* 171 ; and in the same scene,

> And though they shuld match me with power of men,
> Yet doubtfull is the chaunce of battailes ioyned,

with *Thebais* 627-9 :—

> licet omne tecum Graeciae robur trahas
> licet arma longe miles ac late explicet
> fortuna belli semper ancipiti in loco est.

It would perhaps be going too far to connect the lines in Act I. 2 :—

> —Shall bridle so their force of youthfull heates,
> And so restreine the rage of insolence,
> Whiche most assailes the yonge and noble minds

with *Troas* 259 :—

> iuuenile uitium est regere non posse impetum.

But it is at any rate an instance of the dignified expression of commonplace thought, which is one of Seneca's chief characteristics. In *Gorboduc*, as in Seneca, we have moralisings on the impetuosity of youth, the danger of pride, the fixity of fate, the fickleness of fortune, the certainty of death. The mythological allusions in the tragedy are to the infernal company of which Seneca is so fond—Tantalus, Ixion, and the snake-clad furies. The Chorus at the end of Act III is entirely in Seneca's style, and to the same source may be ascribed the rhetorical exaggeration of the speech of Videna which follows. We have also Seneca's over-elaboration and formal preciseness, of which an example may be noted in the pedantic division of the "sortes" of the rebels in the the speech of Eubulus, V. 2.[1]

Tancred, and Gismunda

In the Epistle Dedicatory to *Tancred and Gismund* (acted by the Gentlemen of the Inner Temple in 1568) William Webbe says, "The tragedy was by them most pithily framed, and no less curiously acted in view of her Majesty, by whom it was then as princely accepted, as of the whole honourable audience notably applauded: yea, and of all men generally desired, as a work either in stateliness of show, depth of conceit, or true ornaments of poetical art, inferior to none of the best in that kind: no, were the Roman Seneca the censurer." He therefore commends it "to most men's appetites, who upon our

---

[1] Cf. *Troas* 1088-1097.

experience we know highly to esteem such lofty measures of sententiously composed tragedies." We have here, again, therefore, a tragedy composed in Seneca's style, and built on his model. The dialogue especially reminds us of Seneca by its occasional brilliance, and throughout we have echoes of his thoughts or mode of expression. Renuchio's part in Act V. 1 is evidently modelled on that of the Messenger in the *Thyestes*. Compare the following:—

> Renuchio, is this Salerne I see?
> Doth here King Tancred hold the awful crown?
> Is this the place where civil people be?
> Or do the savage Scythians here abound?

> quaenam ista regio est? Argos et Sparte inpios
> sortita fratres et maris gemini premens
> fauces Corinthos, an feris Hister fugam
> praebens Alanis, an sub aeterna niue
> Hyrcana tellus, an uagi passim Scythae?
>
> (*Thyestes* 627-31).

Then follows in each case a long and elaborate description of the scene and the horrible details of the crime. Compare especially :—

> Cho. O damned deed!
> Ren.   What, deem you this to be
>   All the sad news that I have to unfold?
>   Is here, think you, end of the cruelty
>   That I have seen!
> Cho.   Could any heavier woe
>   Be wrought to him, than to destroy him so?

REN. What, think you this outrage did end so well?
  The horror of the fact, the greatest grief,
  The massacre, the terror is to tell.
CHO. Alack! what could be more? they threw percase
  The dead body to be devour'd and torn
  Of the wild beasts.
REN. Would God it had been cast a savage prey
  To beasts and birds.

CHO. o saeuum scelus.
NVN. exhorruistis? hactenus non stat nefas,
  plus est.
CHO. an ultra maius aut atrocius
  natura recipit?
NVN. sceleris hunc finem putas?
  gradus est.
CHO. quid ultra potuit? obiecit feris
  lanianda forsan corpora atque igne arcuit.
NVN. utinam arcuisset. ne tegat functos humus,
  ne soluat ignis, auibus epulandos licet
  ferisque triste pabulum saeuis trahat.
  (*Thyestes* 743-751).

The Misfortunes of Arthur.

The subject of *The Misfortunes of Arthur*, as of *Gorboduc*, is taken from early British history or legend; but the treatment is entirely after Seneca's manner. Hughes has borrowed not lines merely (these he has borrowed wholesale), but scenes and entire speeches. The first act is little more than a mosaic of extracts from Seneca, pieced together with lines of Hughes's own invention, cast in the style of his model. Gorlois is a ghost after Seneca's own heart, and quotes a number of

lines from the opening speech of the Ghost of Tantalus
in the *Thyestes*. The influence of the same play is
strongly marked in the following scenes, but the model
chiefly followed is now rather the *Agamemnon*, Guenevra
being moulded on Clytemnestra, and Mordred on
Aegisthus. Other plays of Seneca are also laid under
contribution, and Guenevra borrows sentiments from
almost all Seneca's guilty heroes and heroines. Fronia
in Scene ii, and Conan in Scene iv repeat the lines of
the Nurse in the *Agamemnon, Hippolytus, Medea*, and
Hercules Oetaeus, and the Servant in the *Thyestes;* and
Conan also plays the part of Seneca in the *Octavia*. The
speech of the Nuntius, which opens Act II, might be
suggested by the *Agamemnon*, though in Seneca a storm
is described, and here it is a battle. The dialogue
between Mordred and Conan in Scene ii on kingly
rights and duties is borrowed partly from that between
Seneca and Nero in the *Octavia*, partly from that between
Agamemnon and Pyrrhus in the *Troas*, with a few lines
from the *Thyestes*, the *Hippolytus*, and the *Thebais*. In
Scene iii there are considerable extracts from the *Hercules
Furens, Oedipus, Thyestes, Thebais,* and *Hippolytus*. In
Scene iv Hughes breaks away at last from his model,
but not entirely, and the Chorus which follows is
altogether in Seneca's vein. Arthur's speeches in
III. 1 are considerably indebted to the reflections
of Agamemnon in *Troas* 267-283, and it is not
until Scene iii that the author trusts entirely to his
own powers. Arthur's speech is full of pathos and force,
and the speeches that follow are also vigorous, though

suffering from Seneca's fault of rhetorical exaggeration. The last scene has a few excerpts from Seneca, and so has the Chorus, but the latter is in the main original. The rest of the play contains a number of borrowed lines, but nothing like the proportion of the first two acts. The best idea of the extent of the author's indebtedness to Seneca will be gained from Appendix II, where it is set out at length.

Classical Tragedy in England.

The above tragedies were all performed before restricted audiences, though they were afterwards given to the world through the printing-press. *Gorboduc* formed part of the Christmas Festivities of the Gentlemen of the Inner Temple in 1561, and was acted by them on January 18th before the Queen at Whitehall; a piratical issue appeared in 1565, and an authorised edition in 1571. *Tancred and Gismund* was acted before the Queen at the Inner Temple in 1568, and printed in 1591. *The Misfortunes of Arthur* was " presented to her Majestie by the Gentlemen of Grayes Inne, at her Highnesse Court in Greenewich, the twenty eighth day of Februarie in the thirtieth yeare of her Majesties most happy Raigne;" it was printed in the same year (1587-8). These three plays, together with Gascoigne's *Jocasta*, are the earliest known examples of classical tragedy in the English language. As such, they have an interest of their own; but they are chiefly of importance because of the influence they exercised upon plays intended for the popular stage. Later examples of classical tragedy did not exercise this influence, and may be dealt with very briefly. Mr. Symonds has shown[1] that the example of Seneca moulded the *Alaham* and *Mustapha* of Fulke Greville, Lord Brooke, printed in 1633, but written much earlier. It would be easy to enlarge on the indebtedness of these tragedies to Seneca; but they may be dismissed with the remark of Mr. Symonds that "they had no influence over the developement of the English drama, and must be regarded in the light of ponderous literary studies." This is also true of the four *Monarchicke Tragedies* of William Alexander, Earl of Stirling (printed 1603-5). In the plays of both these noblemen we have long passages of meditation varied by philosophic choruses and dialogues of stichomythia. Seneca's influence is also paramount in the *Cleopatra* (1594) and *Philotas* (1605) of Samuel Daniel—works of much greater literary value than the preceding, for Daniel has, to use the words of Mr. Saintsbury,[2] an "almost unsurpassed faculty of ethical verse." But *Cleopatra* and *Philotas* "stand practically alone"[3] in the English drama as studies after the manner of the French school of Seneca, and though interesting as a literary curiosity, they are of no great importance either on the ground of their intrinsic literary merits, or the influence they exercised.

---

[1] *Shakspere's Predecessors*, p. 222.
[2] In a *Preliminary Note on the Position of Daniel's Tragedies in English Literature*, in Vol. III. of Grosart's Edition of Daniel.
[3] Kyd's *Cornelia* (as Mr. Saintsbury points out) and the Countess of Pembroke's *Antony* were merely translations.

The Popular Stage.

Cambyses.

The main stream of English tragedy was flowing in quite other channels. Seneca's influence was felt, but the chief motive was to please a popular audience, which made complete submission to Seneca's authority impossible. The combination of the two impulses was difficult, and at first the connection between the classical and the popular drama was very slight. The "lamentable tragedy" of *Cambyses*,[1] probably contemporary with *Gorboduc*, shews few marks of classical influence; it is "mixed full of pleasant mirth," and has much in common with the moralities; but there is a curious prologue appealing to the authority of Agathon and Seneca :—

> The sage and witty Seneca
>   His words thereto did frame;
> The honest exercise of kings
>   Men will ensue the same.
> But contrary-wise, if that a king
>   Abuse his kingly seat,
> His ignomy and bitter shame
>   In fine shall be more great.

The reference seems to be to *Thyestes* 213-7 :—

> rex uelit honesta: nemo non eadem uolet.
> ....ubi non est pudor,
> nec cura iuris, sanctitas pietas fides :
> instabile regnum est.

---

[1] One cannot say positively that *Cambyses* was written for the popular stage; but in spite of the fact that the author, Thomas Preston, was a fellow of King's College, Cambridge, and acted at the University before Queen Elizabeth, I am inclined to believe that, like *Appius and Virginia*, it was performed on the "scaffold" of the miracle plays; on the title page there is no mention of its being acted on any special occasion, as in the case of the early tragedies mentioned above.

Damon and Pithias (pr. 1571) also contains much that is *Damon and Pithias* alien to Seneca; it is a "tragical comedy" and the humours of Grim the Collier are neither tragic nor classical; but in the serious part of the drama there is an attempt—not a very successful one—to imitate the manner of Seneca. The scene between Dionysius and Eubulus is pretty closely modelled on that between Nero and Seneca in the *Octavia*, e.g. :—

> DION. A mild prince the people despiseth.
> EUB. A cruel king the people hateth.
> DION. Let them hate me, so they fear me.
> EUB. That is not the way to live in safety.
> DION. My sword and my power shall purchase my quietness.
> EUB. That is sooner procured by mercy and gentleness.
> DION. Dionysius ought to be feared.
> EUB. Better for him to be well beloved.

> NERO. calcat iacentem uulgus.
> SEN.   inuisum opprimit.
> NERO. ferrum tuetur principem.
> SEN.   melius fides.
> NERO. decet timeri Caesarem.
> SEN.   at plus diligi.
>   (*Octavia* 467-9.)

And again :—

> DION. Fortune maketh all things subject to my power.
> EUB. Believe her not, she is a light goddess; she can laugh and low'r.

> NERO. fortuna nostra cuncta permittit mihi.
> SEN. crede obsequenti parcius. leuis est dea.
>   (*Octavia* 463-4.)

The Spanish Tragedy.   The *Spanish Tragedy* (pr. 1599, acted probably about 1588) is important from its popularity and its typical character. Some of the points of contact with Seneca have been noticed already; we have also quotations and translations from Seneca of no great moment.¹ The chief significance of the play lies in its developement of the bloody horrors detailed by the Ghost at the end of the action :—

> Ay, now my hopes have end in their effects,
> When blood and sorrow finish my desires :
> Horatio murder'd in his father's bower ;
> Vild Serberine by Pedringano slain ;
> False Pedringano hang'd by quaint device ;
> Fair Isabella by herself misdone ;
> Prince Balthazar by Bell'-Imperia stabb'd ;
> The Duke of Castile and his wicked son
> Both done to death by old Hieronimo.
> My Bell'-Imperia fall'n, as Dido fell :
> And good Hieronimo slain by himself.

But, in spite of all this bloodshed, the distinctive features of Seneca's mode of treatment are wanting.

MARLOWE.   It was MARLOWE's¹ self-appointed task to win the popular ear

> From jigging veins of rhyming mother wits,
> And such conceits as clownage keeps in pay

to the " high astounding terms " of the stately classical drama. In making the change—one of tremendous

---

¹ See Appendix I.

importance for the English drama—he would naturally select those features of classical tragedy which would appeal most readily to popular favour. Seneca's bombast and violence the multitude could understand; but they would not submit to his philosophical disquisitions. Accordingly we find in Marlowe few of the sage reflections with which Seneca adorned his plays; but we have all Seneca's horror of incident and exaggeration of expression. What Ulrici says of Marlowe accurately describes Seneca's tragic style: "In his hand, the forcible becomes the forced, the uncommon the unnatural, whereas the grand and sublime degenerate into the grotesque and monstrous. .... the tragic element almost invariably degenerates into the horrible; with him the essence of tragedy does not consist in the fall of the truly noble, great and lovely, as occasioned by their own weakness, one-sideness and want of freedom, but in the annihilating conflict of the primary elements of human nature, the blind struggle between the most vehement emotions and passions."[1] Ulrici may be deemed a prejudiced critic; but Mr. J. A. Symonds will assuredly not be accused of any lack of appreciation. He says of *Tamburlaine*: "Blood flows in rivers. Shrieks and groans and curses mingle with heaven-defying menaces and ranting vaunts. The action is one tissue of violence and horror." Mr. Symonds modifies this unfavourable judgement with the remark that "Marlowe has succeeded in saving his hero,

---

[1] *Shakspeare's Dramatic Art*, translated by L. Dora Schmitz (1876), I. 152.

amid all his 'lunes,' from caricature, by the inbreathed spirituality with which he sustains his madness at its height;" and what is true to some extent of Marlowe's bombast is still more true of his use of the horrible. Where Seneca would be simply disgusting, Marlowe reaches the topmost height of tragic power; in *Edward II*, V. 5, for instance, as Dr. Ward remarks, "the unutterable horror of the situation is depicted without our sense of the loathsome being aroused." Marlowe, indeed, was immeasureably superior to Seneca, both as a poet and a dramatist, and in his hands the very crudities and faults of the tragic model of his age were transformed by the transcendant power of genius till they often become sublime and beautiful. Even where, as in the bombast of *Tamburlaine*, the defect is only hidden, not removed, by the genuine poetic spirit inbreathed into the whole, the error was of such a character as rather to commend itself than otherwise to the audience of that day, with its lust for violence and horror; and Seneca may fairly claim some portion of the fame which *Tamburlaine* has won as "a dramatic poem which intoxicated the audience of the London play-houses with indescribable delight, and which inaugurated a new epoch'"[1] in the history of the English drama.

PEELE. Dr. Ward observes that PEELE's *Battle of Alcazar* "naturally suggests a comparison with *Tamburlaine*, which it resembles in the extravagance of expression—indeed

---

[1] *Shakspere's Predecessors*, p. 628.

the rant—with which it abounds;" and it is perhaps rather to the influence of Marlowe than of Seneca that we should ascribe the resemblances to the style of the Roman tragedies to be found in Peele. It should be noted, however, that in the prologue to *The Arraignment of Paris* (pr. 1584), we have already a specimen of that grandiloquent blank verse with which *Tamburlaine* (pr. 1590, acted before 1587) caught the popular ear:—

> Condemned soul, Ate, from lowest hell,
> And deadly rivers of th' infernal Jove,
> Where bloodless ghosts in pains of endless date
> Fill ruthless ears with never-ceasing cries,
> Behold, I come......

Peele is excessively fond of the infernal machinery which Seneca so often brought into play, and in *The Battle of Alcazar* he uses it again and again, without any regard to its appropiateness. Take for instance the last speech of the Moor:—

> Mount me I will:
> But may I never pass the river, till I be
> Revenged upon thy soul, accursed Abdelmelec!
> If not on earth, yet when we meet in hell, \/
> Before grim Minos, Rhadamanth, and Aeacus,
> The combat will I crave upon thy ghost,
> And drag thee thorough the loathsome pools
> Of Lethes, Styx, and fiery Phlegethon.

In this play Peele carried Marlowe's bombast beyond incoherence into positive nonsense, as in Act I. 2:—

THE MOOR. Away, and let me hear no more of this.
Why, boy,
Are we successors to the great Abdallas
Descended from th' Arabian Muly Xarif,
And shall we be afraid of Bassas and of bugs,
Rawhead and Bloodybone? [1]

Peele has Seneca's gruesomeness without Marlowe's delicacy of treatment. In *David and Bethsabe* Joab thus delivers himself as to the dead Absalom:—

Night-ravens and owls shall ring his fatal knell,
And sit exclaiming on his damned soul;
There shall they heap their preys of carrion,
Till all his grave be clad with stinking bones,
That it may loathe the sense of every man.

Peele's imitation of Seneca's dialogue has been already noted. [2]

GREENE.

GREENE[3] imitated Marlowe's bombastic style, not very successfully, in *Alphonsus, King of Arragon;* but violence and extravagance of diction were alien to the spirit of his muse, for of all the predecessors of Shakspere he had the lightest touch and the freshest fancy, bringing out with ease and naturalness the humour and pathos that lie in simple folk and ordinary situations. What he

---

[1] In this and the preceding quotation I have adopted the reading of Mr. A. H. Bullen's edition.
[2] See p. 21.
[3] Greene took the title and the text of his prose tract, *Never too Late,* from *Agamemnon* 244:—
Nam sera nunquam est ad bonos mores uia.

did borrow of Seneca was not to his advantage. The unseasonable employment of Latin mythology, which Mr. Symonds notes as Greene's main stylistic defect, should probably be laid to the joint account of Seneca and Ovid; Hercules especially is introduced with painful frequency. The same fault is to be seen in *The First Part of the Tragicall Raigne of King Selimus* (pr. 1594), which Dr. Grosart includes in his edition of Greene's works. If this play is rightly ascribed to Greene, it has an interest apart from its intrinsic merits. It bears too plainly the stamp of *Tamburlaine* not to have been written after that epoch-making drama, but the frequency of rhymed lines and other marks of style would fix it as one of Greene's earlier plays. It contains some of the curious similes after Lyly's manner which form one of the most striking characteristics of Greene's earlier prose style, and are also to be found, though to a very much less extent, in his tragedies.[1] In *Selimus* we have the " subtill " Crocodile, the Phoenix, the Echinaeis, the " craftie " Polypus, the Ibis, the Basilisk, and the Cockatrice. All these curious creatures are to be found in Greene's prose works or tragedies, the Echinaeis being identified by Grosart with the Echinus of *Alphonsus*. If we may take it as established that this is an early play of Greene's, we have the interesting fact that Seneca exerted considerable influence upon his style in the early part of his career. An examination of *Selimus* shows that the author was greatly influenced by Seneca. The play opens with reflections

King Selimus.

---
[1] *e. g. Alphonsus* (Grosart) Vol. xiii., p. 343, lines 308-19; p. 355, ll. 618-20.

on the cares and uncertainty of empire quite in the style
of the Roman dramatist and philosopher. The description of the golden age may be paralleled by *Hippolytus*
533-557; and the sceptical reasoning that follows by
Troas 380-417. Then we have Sisyphus, Ixion, and
"the cave of damned ghoasts" with which Seneca has
made us familiar, and later on we are confronted by "all
the damned monsters of black hell." Seneca's dialogue
is successfully imitated, and sometimes not only the
style, but the matter also is borrowed :—

    AGA. Do you not feare the people's aduerse fame?
    ACO. It is the greatest glorie of a king
           When, though his subjects hate his wicked deeds,
           Yet are they forst to beare them all with praise.
    AGA. Whom feare constraines to praise their princes deeds,
           That feare, eternall hatred in them feeds.
    ACO. He knowes not how to sway the kingly mace,
           That loues to be great in his peoples grace :
           The surest ground for kings to build vpon,
           Is to be fear'd and curst of euery one.
           What, though the world of nations me hate?
           Hate is peculiar to a princes state.
    AGA. Where ther's no shame, no care of holy law,
           No faith, no iustice, no integritie,
           That state is full of mutabilitie.
    ACO. Bare faith, pure vertue, poore integritie,
           Are ornaments fit for a priuate man ;
           Beseemes a prince for to do all he can.

Compare with this *Thyestes* 204-218 :—

    SAT.   fama te populi nihil
        aduersa terret?

ATR.   maximum hoc regni bonum est,
        quod facta domini cogitur populus sui
        quam ferre tam laudare.
SAT.   quos cogit metus
        laudare, eosdem reddit inimicos metus.
        at qui fauoris gloriam ueri petit,
        animo magis quam uoce laudari uolet.
ATR.   laus uera et humili saepe contingit uiro,
        non nisi potenti falsa. quod nolunt, uelint.
SAT.   rex uelit honesta : nemo non eadem uolet.
ATR.   vbicumque tantum honesta dominanti licent,
        precario regnatur.
SAT.   ubi non est pudor,
        nec cura iuris, sanctitas pietas fides :
        instabile regnum est.
ATR.   sanctitas pietas fides
        priuata bona sunt, qua iuuat reges eant.

Lines 1165-8 (p. 239) may be compared with *Hercules Oetaeus* 143-6, and 1354-5 (p. 246) with *Hercules Furens* 517. The praises of a country life on p. 270 may have been suggested by *Hercules Furens* 160-4. Some of the situations may also have been suggested by Seneca, but this is more doubtful. The young Mahomet, like Astyanax in the *Troas*, is cast down from an "ayrie toure," but with this additional horror, that a "groue of steele-head speares" is prepared for his reception. In spite of this refinement of cruelty, the youth meets death with no less hardihood than the son of Hector :—

> Thou shalt not fear me, Acomat, with death,
> Nor will I beg my pardon at thy hands.
> But as thou giu'st me such a monstrous death,
> So do I freely leaue to thee my curse.

The princess Solyma is equally brave; she prays to be slain before her husband Mustaffa, that she may not see his death; Amphitryon in the *Hercules Furens* asks a like boon from Lycus with respect to Megara and her children.

SHAKSPERE. SHAKSPERE undoubtedly fell under the influence both of the rhetorical drama of which Marlowe was the father and master, and of the "tragedy of blood" which is perhaps better represented by Kyd's *Spanish Tragedy*; but whether Shakspere was directly indebted to Seneca is a question as difficult as it is interesting. As English tragedy advances, there grows up an accumulation of Seneca influence within the English drama in addition to the original source, and it becomes increasingly difficult to distinguish between the direct and the indirect influence of Seneca. In no case is the difficulty greater than in that of Shakspere. Of Marlowe, Jonson, Chapman, Marston, and Massinger we can say with certainty that they read Seneca, and reproduced their reading in their tragedies; of Middleton and Heywood we can say with almost equal certainty that they give no sign of direct indebtedness to Seneca, and that they probably came only under the indirect influence through the imitations of their predecessors and contemporaries. In the case of Shakspere we cannot be absolutely certain either way. Professor Baynes thinks that it is probable that Shakspere read Seneca at school; and even if he did not, we may be sure that at some period of his career he would turn to the generally accepted model of classical tragedy, either in the original or in the translation. The decision must, however, rest upon the internal evidence contained in the plays themselves, and while I look upon this as pointing very plainly to an almost certain conclusion, it can hardly be said to amount to absolute proof. A number of instances have been already quoted in which Shakspere might have been influenced by the example of Seneca; and others will be given; but it cannot be said that in any one case the resemblance is absolutely convincing. The evidence must be taken in its cumulative force, and that must be my excuse if I have quoted some parallels that are not very obvious. Another scrap of evidence is to be found in Shakspere's mythology. It might seem absurd to *Mythology.* attach any importance to the fact that Hercules, Seneca's favourite hero, is mentioned by Shakspere about fifty times; but it is at any rate not without significance when an obscure character such as Lichas is referred to at the same time, as in *The Merchant of Venice*, II. 1 and *Antony and Cleopatra*, IV. 12. The latter passage is perhaps worth quoting:—

> The shirt of Nessus is upon me: Teach me,
> Alcides, thou mine ancestor, thy rage:
> Let me lodge Lichas on the horns o' the moon;
> And with those hands, that grasp'd the heaviest club,
> Subdue my worthiest self.

At first sight it seems more than likely that this is from Seneca; but it might also come from Ovid.

Whether Shakspere used the translation of 1581 is a further problem, depending on the solution of the first A passage in *King John*, III. 4 :—

> A sceptre snatch'd with an unruly hand
> Must be as boisterously maintain'd as gain'd ;
> And he that stands upon a slippery place
> Makes nice of no vile hold to stay him up.

is not unlike *Hercules Furens* 345-9 :—

> rapta sed trepida manu
> sceptra optinentur.   omnis in ferro est salus.
> quod ciuibus tenere te inuitis scias,
> strictus tuetur ensis.   alieno in loco
> haut stabile regnum est.

If the reader decides that the resemblance is so close as to imply direct connection, the conclusion may be drawn that Shakspere used the original, and not the translation, which gives quite a different rendering of the text :—

> ———but got with fearful hand
> My sceptors are obtaynd : in sword doth all my safety stand.
> What thee thou wotst agaynst the will of cytesyns to get,
> The bright drawne sword must it defend : in forrayne countrey set
> No stable kingdome is.

The Shaksperean "maintain" is more correct than the professed translation ; Pierrot shows that *optinentur* $=$ *retinentur, seruantur*. The Shaksperean version of *trepida manu* is more doubtful, but it is supported by some authorities. Pierrot quotes a paraphrase which runs,

"Qui genus iactat suum, aliena laudat; at qui sceptrum rapuit, ei laborandum et uigilandum est, ut ui partum ui retineat."

The problem of Shakspere's relation to Seneca is further complicated by questions of authorship. If we could accept *Titus Andronicus* as written wholly by Shakspere, all difficulty would be at an end, for the Latin quotations from Seneca[1] set every doubt at rest. Even without this direct testimony, the internal evidence is sufficiently striking. The subject and style of the tragedy are thoroughly Senecan. It is made up of

> murders, rapes, and massacres,
> Acts of black night, abominable deeds,
> Complots of mischief, treason, villanies. (V. 1)

No detail of physical horror is spared; from beginning to end the stage reeks with blood, and the characters vie with one another in barbarity. Even the gentle Lavinia helps to prepare the Thyestean banquet; and Titus and his sons are no less eager for revenge, and no less cruel in its execution, than Tamora and Aaron. The style exaggerates even these heaped-up horrors, and the passions are often strained to artificiality. The descriptions of rural life and scenery, which relieve the sanguinary picture to some extent, are not strange to Seneca. The

---
[1] See Appendix I.

hunting scene (II. 2) might be suggested by the opening' of the *Hippolytus*, and the lines in II. 3 :—

> The birds chant melody on every bush ;
> The snake lies rolled in the cheerful sun ;
> The green leaves quiver with the cooling wind,

may be compared with *Hippolytus* 516-8 :—

> hic aues querulae fremunt
> ramique uentis lene percussi tremunt
> ueteresque fagi.

The description of the "barren detested vale," the scene of the murder of Bassianus and the rape of Lavinia, reminds us of the place where Atreus sacrificed his nephews. *Thyestes* 650-5 :—

> arcana in imo regia recessu patet,
> alta uetustum ualle conpescens nemus,
> penetrale regni, nulla qua laetos solet
> praebere ramos arbos aut ferro coli,
> sed taxus et cupressus et nigra ilice
> obscura nutat silua.

> The trees, though summer, yet forlorn and lean,
> O'ercome with moss and baleful mistletoe :
> Here never shines the sun ; here nothing breeds,
> Unless the nightly owl or fatal raven.

For the last touch in this dark picture see *Hercules Furens* 690-2 :—

> palus inertis foeda Cocyti iacet.
> hic uultur illic luctifer bubo gemit
> omenque tristis resonat infaustae strigis.

> They told me, here, at dead time of the night,
> A thousand fiends, a thousand hissing snakes,
> Ten thousand swelling toads, as many urchins,
> Would make such fearful and confused cries,
> As any mortal body hearing it
> Should straight fall mad, or else die suddenly.

So *Thyestes* 668-673 :—

> hic nocte tota gemere feralis deos
> fama est, catenis lucus excussis sonat
> ululantque manes. quicquid audire est metus,
> illic uidetur: errat antiquis uetus
> emissa bustis turba et insultant loco
> maiora notis monstra.

Among minor dramatic devices used by Seneca we may note Lavinia's plea for death, and Quintus and Martius's presentiment of coming destruction (II. 3). Seneca's reflective tendency is strongly marked in this play, and we have a number of "brief sententious precepts" like those with which Seneca adorned his gruesome themes. Tamora's plea (I. 1) :—

> Andronicus, stain not thy tomb with blood.
> Wilt thou draw near the nature of the gods?
> Draw near them then in being merciful:
> Sweet mercy is nobility's true badge.

may be compared with the considerations urged by Agamemnon on a like occasion, when Pyrrhus sought to appease his father's ghost by the sacrifice of Polyxena. Compare also the passage (I. 1) :—

> In peace and honour rest you here, my sons;
> Rome's readiest champions, repose you here in rest,
> Secure from wordly chances and mishaps!
> Here lurks no treason, here no envy swells,
> Here grow no damned drugs;[1] here are no storms,
> No noise, but silence and eternal sleep:
> In peace and honour rest you here, my sons!

with the Chorus in the *Troas* 151-6, 166-8:—

> FELIX PRIAMUS dicite cunctae.
> liber manes uadit ad imos
> nec feret umquam
> uincta Graium ceruice iugum.
> non ille duos uidit Atridas
> nec fallacem cernit Vlixem.
> ....
> nunc elysii nemoris tutus
> errat in umbris
> interque pias felix animas
> Hectora quaerit. FELIX PRIAMUS.

It is remarkable that the passages which challenge comparison with Seneca are the very ones in which we should be readiest to recognize the hand of Shakspere.

Henry VI

Critical difficulties again confront us in the consideration of the three parts of *Henry VI*, and *Richard III;* but the opinions of competent critics differ so widely that it would be useless for me to enter into the discussion as to the authorship of *Henry VI*, and the relation thereto of the

---

[1] I adhere, as elsewhere, to the text of *The Cambridge Shakespeare*; "grudges" seems to me the better reading.

two parts of *The Contention between the two Famous Houses of York and Lancaster*. It would be equally unwise for me to attempt to set at rest the doubts recently raised by James Russell Lowell[1] as to the authorship of *Richard III*; I *Richard III and Richard III*. have nothing of importance to add to the evidence of genuinenesss, and what I have to say as to the connection with Seneca would probably lead critics of different views to different inferences. I am, however, concerned, not with the conclusions that may be drawn, but with the fact that *Henry VI* (especially Part iii) and *Richard III* have much in common with Seneca. They are pervaded by the ruthless spirit of violence and bloodshed, and abound in the crude horrors of physical repulsiveness, such as the bringing of Suffolk's mutilated body on to the stage (2 *Henry VI*, IV. 1), and the subsequent introduction of Queen Margaret with the head in her hands (IV. 4). Iden brings on the stage Cade's head (2 *Henry VI*, V. 1), and Richard that of Somerset (3. I. 1). All through *The Third Part of Henry VI*, and *Richard III*, the slaughter is continuous, and accompanied by circumstances of great inhumanity, as witness the mock crowning of York before his death, and the murders of Rutland and the young Prince of Wales. The murder of the young princes in *Richard III* is only narrated, and the executions in this play generally take place off the stage, only Clarence and Richard himself dying in sight of the audience; but the personages of the drama move in the same atmosphere of blood, and Richard above all sustains

---

[1] In an article in the *Atlantic Monthly* for December, 1891.

to the full his character of fiendish cruelty. He has the vindictiveness, the intellectual force, the undaunted spirit, the ruthless cruelty, the absolute lack of moral feeling of Seneca's Medea, coupled with the haughtiness of Eteocles, and the bloody hypocrisy of Atreus; as with Seneca's heroic criminals, his passions know no bounds—he is not human, but praeternatural. And what is true, in its fullest sense, of the "cacodaemon," Richard, is true in a less degree of the minor characters. Queen Margaret and Clifford vie with Richard himself in merciless cruelty. Edward, then Earl of March, says in 3 *Henry VI*, I. 2 :—

> But for a kingdom any oath may be broken :
> I would break a thousand oaths to reign one year.

just as Polynices, under similar circumstances, says in *Thebais* 664 :—

> imperia pretio quolibet constant bene.

The same exaggeration of expression is to be noted in the next scene, where Clifford says to Rutland :—

> Had I thy brethren here, their lives and thine
> Were not revenge sufficient for me ;
> No, if I digg'd up thy forefathers' graves,
> And hung their rotten coffins up in chains,
> It could not slake mine ire, nor ease my heart.
> The sight of any of the house of York
> Is as a fury to torment my soul ;
> And till I root out their accursed line
> And leave not one alive, I live in hell.

Even the quiet Henry gives way to the prevailing

exaggeration of tone when he falls in love, and expresses his passion with the ardour of a Phaedra. 1 *Henry VI*, V. 5:—

> Your wondrous rare description, noble earl,
> Of beauteous Margaret hath astonish'd me:
> Her virtues graced with external gifts
> Do breed love's settled passions in my heart:
> And like as rigour of tempestuous gusts
> Provokes the mightiest hulk against the tide,
> So am I driven by breath of her renown,
> Either to suffer shipwreck or arrive
> Where I may have fruition of her love.

This "wind and tide" metaphor is a favourite one with both Seneca and Shakspere. In the two following passages it is substantially the same. 3 *Henry VI*, II. 5:

> This battle fares like to the morning's war,
> When dying clouds contend with growing light,
> ....
> Now sways it this way, like a mighty sea
> Forced by the tide to combat with the wind;
> Now sways it that way, like the selfsame sea
> Forced to retire by fury of the wind:
> Sometime the flood prevails, and then the wind;
> Now one the better, then another best;
> Both tugging to be victors, breast to breast,
> Yet neither conqueror nor conquered.

>   fluctibus uariis agor,
> ut, cum hinc profundum uentus hinc aestus rapit,
> incerta dubitat unda cui cedat malo.
>   (*Agamemnon* 139-141.)

In this case it seems worth while to subjoin Studley's translation (pub. 1566):—

> As when here wynd, and their the streame when both their force
>   wil try,
> From sandes alow doth hoyst and reare the seas with surges hye.
> The waltring waue doth staggeryng stand not weting what to do,
> But (houeryng) doubtes, whose furious force he best may yeld
>   him to.

Compare also 3 *Henry VI*, II. 6:—

> As doth a sail, fill'd with a fretting gust,
> Command an argosy to stem the waves.

with *Hippolytus* 186-9, and *Thyestes* 438-9.

Some of Seneca's leading ideas are repeatedly reproduced in these plays. All the more important characters are tinged with Seneca's Stoical fatalism. His "fatis agimur, cedite fatis" is expressed by King Edward in 3 *Henry VI*, IV. 3, with the metaphor just spoken of:

> What fates impose, that men must needs abide;
> It boots not to resist both wind and tide.

So too Queen Margaret in 3 *Henry VI*, V. 4:—

> What cannot be avoided
> 'Twere childish weakness to lament or fear.

and Richard, in the course of a dialogue containing many examples of Senecan stichomythia (*Richard III*, IV. 4), says with all the impressive conciseness of the Roman dramatist and philosopher—

> All unavoided is the doom of destiny.

The cares and risks of high places and the benefits of obscurity are urged as frequently in these plays as in the tragedies of Seneca, and in much the same strain. Queen Margaret's words in *Richard III*, I. 3 :—

> They that stand high have many blasts to shake them.

may be compared with *Hippolytus* 1136-1140, *Agamemnon* 57-9, and *Oedipus* 6-11. Henry resigns the crown, as he says (3. IV. 6)—

> that I may conquer fortune's spite
> By living low, where fortune cannot hurt me.

Compare *Hercules Furens* 201-4, and *Hercules Oetaeus* 701-3. A much longer and more important passage— too long for quotation—in 3 *Henry VI*, II. 5, describing the advantages of a shepherd's life over a king's, may be compared with *Hippolytus* 516-533, *Thyestes* 450-3, and *Hercules Oetaeus* 647-661; and Henry's words on true kingship (3. III. 1) remind us of *Thyestes* 388-390.

Another idea frequently put forward by Seneca and by Shakspere is that of the presentiment of evil.[1] We have a fairly close parallel in *Richard III*, II. 3 :—

> By a divine instinct men's minds mistrust
> Ensuing dangers; as, by proof, we see
> The waters swell before a boisterous storm.

---

[1] See *Thyestes* 417-490 and 946-973; *Hercules Oetaeus* 720-5. We have the same idea in *Romeo and Juliet* I. 4, *ad fin.* and III. 5 ; and *Richard II*, II 2.

and *Thyestes* 901-4:—

> mittit luctus signa futuri
> mens ante sui presaga mali,
> instat nautis fera tempestas,
> cum sine uento tranquilla tument.

To this may be added another commonplace of morality which occurs more than once in each poet. *Richard III*, IV. 2:—

> Uncertain way of gain! But I am in
> So far in blood that sin will pluck on sin.

Agamemnon 116:—

> per scelera semper sceleribus tutum est iter.

Theodor Vatke [1] has suggested a comparison between the wooing of Lady Anne by Gloucester and that of Megara by Lycus. In the same way we might seek a parallel for the conjuration of the Spirit in 2 *Henry VI*, I. 4 in the raising of the shade of Laius; and in the same passage from the *Oedipus* we might endeavour to discover a suggestion of the appearance of the ghosts in Clarence's dream. But how wide is the gulf between the mythical figures of Seneca and the living spirits of Shakspere; instead of Zethus and Amphion, Niobe and Agave, we have the ghosts of those whom Clarence had wronged, among them

> A shadow like an angel, with bright hair
> Dabbled in blood; and he squeak'd out aloud,

---

[1] *Jahrbuch der Deutschen Shakespeare Gesellschaft*, IV. p. 64.

> "Clarence is come; false, fleeting, perjured Clarence,
> That stabb'd me in the field by Tewksbury:
> Seize on him, Furies, take him to your torments!"

The difference is so great—it is the world-wide difference between art and artifice—that any slight resemblance is quite overshadowed by our sense of the immeasureable superiority of Shakspere's picture. With more justice, perhaps, we might compare the lament of the Duchess of York (*Richard III*, II. 2):—

> Alas, I am the mother of these moans!
> Their woes are parcell'd, mine are general.
> She for an Edward weeps, and so do I.........

with that of Hecuba in *Troas* 1070-2:—

> quoscumque luctus fleueris, flebis meos.
> sua quemque tantum, me omnium clades premit,
> mihi cuncta pereunt, quisquis est Hecubae est miser.

Hamlet marks the climax of the reflective tendency in Shakspere and in the English drama, though coupled, as in Seneca, with a full complement

> Of carnal, bloody and unnatural acts. (V. 2.)

Knight has observed that in the latter characteristic *Hamlet* is connected with the school of *Titus Andronicus*; but whether this is due to an old *Hamlet* which was not Shakspere's, or the earlier *Hamlet* which is referred to by Nash was written by Shakspere at a time when he was still under the influence of Senecan tragedy, is too large a question to be discussed here. In its ultimate form the play still contains some slight reminiscences of Seneca, though we shall look in vain for the " whole handfulls " of tragical speeches sneered at by Nash as borrowed from the English translation. In Klein's opinion the appearance of the Ghost of Laius in the *Oedipus* forms " no unworthy study " for the famous scene " on the platform before the castle ; " but of Shakspere's ghost-scene there is nothing to be found in Seneca beyond the very baldest suggestion. With greater justice Mr. H. A. J. Munro [1] says that

> the dread of something after death.
> The undiscover'd country from whose bourn
> No traveller returns

has not a little in common with *Hercules Furens* 868-870 and *Hercules Oetaeus* 1529-1531 :—

> sera nos illo referat senectus.
> nemo ad id sero uenit unde numquam,
> cum semel uenit, potuit reuerti.
>
> dic ad aeternos properare manes
> Herculem et regnum canis inquieti
> unde non unquam remeauit ullus.

Indeed the whole of Hamlet's famous soliloquy may be said to arise out of the question in *Troas* 380-1 :—

> verum est, an timidos fabula decipit,
> umbras corporibus uiuere conditis.

---

[1] *Journal of Philology*, VI. p. 70.

Compare also IV. 3

> Diseases desperate grown
> By desperate appliance are relieved,
> Or not at all.

with *Agamemnon* 153-5 :—

CLYT. et ferrum et ignis saepe medicinae loco est.
NVTR. extrema primo nemo temptauit loco.
CLYT. capienda rebus in malis praeceps uia est.

We have Seneca's notion of presentiment and his Stoical fatalism in V. 2 :—"if it be now, 'tis not to come; if it be not to come, it will be now; if it be not now, yet it will come : the readiness is all; since no man has aught of what he leaves, what is't to leave betimes?"

It is again the hand of fate, or rather the hand of chance, that brings about the catastrophe, with its "accidental judgements, casual slaughters" and "purposes mistook fall'n on the inventors' heads."

As in *Hamlet*, the reflective element in *Macbeth* arises from no lack of desperate deeds. From the Murder of Duncan, which is described with every detail of horror, there is a continuous outpour of blood until in the last scene the head of Macbeth is brought on the stage. But in *Macbeth*, as in Seneca, we have a horrible theme treated in such a way as to give frequent occasion for deep reflection. It should be noted further that in *Macbeth* Shakspere's reflective tendency is displayed more after the manner of Seneca than in *Hamlet*. Hamlet's fondness for reflection is part —a very important part—of his character. In *Macbeth* the reflections are uttered not by one character alone, but by almost all; and not in long soliloquies, but in brief, pregnant sentences, quite after Seneca's manner. In some instances the ideas expressed bear considerable similarity to those of Seneca. Thus I. 7 :—

> We but teach
> Bloody instructions, which being taught return
> To plague the inventor: this even-handed justice
> Commends the ingredients of our poison'd chalice
> To our own lips.

> quod quisque fecit, patitur. auctorem scelus
> repetit suoque premitur exemplo nocens.
> *(Hercules Furens* 739-740.)

IV. 3.:— Give sorrow words: the grief that does not speak
Whispers the o'erfraught heart, and bids it break.

> curae leues loquuntur ingentes stupent.
> *(Hippolytus* 615.)

V. 3:— I have lived long enough: my way of life
Is fall'n into the sear, the yellow leaf,
And that which should accompany old age,
As honour, love, obedience, troops of friends,
I must not look to have.

> cur animam in ista luce detineam amplius
> morerque nihil est. cuncta iam amisi bona:
> mentem arma famam coniugem gnatos manus
> etiam furorem. *(Hercules Furens* 1265-8.)

Compare further the lines that follow

> Canst thou not minister to a mind diseased.........

with the continuation of the passage in *Hercules Furens* :—

> nemo polluto queat
> animo mederi.[1]

IV. 2 :— Things at the worst will cease, or else climb upward
To what they were before

with *Thebais* 198-9 :—

> cuius haud ultra mala
> exire possunt in loco tuto est situs.

and *Oedipus* 855 :—

> tuto mouetur quicquid extremo in loco est.

II. 4 :— Thou see'st, the heavens, as troubled with man's act,
Threaten his bloody stage : by the clock 'tis day
And yet dark night strangles the travelling lamp :
Is't night's predominance, or the day's shame,
That darkness does the face of earth entomb,
When living light should kiss it ?

We have the same idea in *Agamemnon* 763-4 :—

> fugit lux alma et obscurat genas
> nox alta et aether obditus tenebris latet.

and in the fourth Chorus of the *Thyestes*.

Compare also the apostrophe to sleep in II. 2 with

---

[1] The Doctor in *Two Noble Kinsmen*, IV. 3, says "I think she has a perturbed minde, which I cannot minister to."

Hercules Furens 1071-1081, and note the splendid developement of the eulogy of the rest of the grave, already remarked in *Titus Andronicus* :—

> Duncan is in his grave;
> After life's fitful fever he sleeps well;
> Treason has done his worst: nor steel, nor poison,
> Malice domestic, foreign levy, nothing,
> Can touch him further.

Then we have II. 1 :—

> Will all great Neptune's ocean wash this blood
> Clean from my hand?

> quis eluet me Tanais? aut quae barbaris
> maeotis undis pontico incumbens mari?
> non ipse toto magnus oceano pater
> tantum expiarit sceleris. (*Hippolytus* 723-6).

> quis Tanais aut quis Nilus aut quis persica
> uiolentus unda Tigris aut Rhenus ferox
> Tagusue hibera turbidus gaza fluens,
> abluere dextram poterit? arctoum licet
> Maeotis in me gelida transfundat mare
> et tota Tethys per meas currat manus:
> haerebit altum facinus. (*Hercules Furens* 1330-6.)

The last is a parallel which has attracted the attention of many readers of Seneca and Shakspere, and was apparently first placed on record by Lessing in the *Theatralische Bibliothek* (1754). It may be, too, that in this passage of Seneca Shakspere found the suggestion of that blood-

stained little hand which forms so impressive a feature
in the famous sleep-walking scene.¹

King Lear is further removed than *Macbeth* from the **King Lear.**
spirit of Senecan tragedy; but, in addition to wholesale
slaughter and physical horrors such as the putting out of
Gloster's eyes, it contains some resemblances worth
noting. We have Seneca's hopeless fatalism, not only in
the catastrophe, but repeatedly brought forward in the
course of the play. Gloster in his blindness says
(IV. I) :—

> As flies to wanton boys are we to the gods;
> They kill us for their sport.

Kent in IV. 3 :—

> It is the stars,
> The stars above us, govern our conditions.

---

¹ The idea was probably suggested to Seneca by Aeschylus *Choephoroe*
63-5, which is so corrupt in the sole authoritative MS. now extant that
only the general drift of the passage can be determined. Plumptre's
translation runs :—

> and water streams,
> Though all in common course
> Should flow to cleanse the guilt
> Of murder that the sin-stained hand defiles,
> Would yet flow all in vain
> That guilt to purify.

Paley in a note says " there can be no doubt..........that *water* is
meant, the usual purification in murder." See also Sophocles *Ajax*
654-6, and the Scholiast's Note thereon, stating that it was the custom
of the ancients to cleanse the pollution of murder by washing the
hands. Cf. Ovid *Fasti* II. 45-6 :—

> Ah nimium faciles, qui tristia crimina caedis
> Fluminea tolli posse putetis aqua.

and Edgar in V. 2 :—

> Men must endure
> Their going hence, even as their coming hither:
> Ripeness is all.

Compare also III. 6 :—

> When we our betters see bearing our woes,
> We scarcely think our miseries our foes.
> Who alone suffers, suffers most i' the mind;
> Leaving free things, and happy shows, behind:
> But then the mind much suffering doth o'er-skip,
> When grief hath mates, and bearing fellowship.

with *Troas* 1019-1035; and IV. 1 :—

> To be worst,
> The lowest and most dejected thing of fortune,
> Stands still in esperance, lives not in fear:
> The lamentable change is from the best,
> The worst returns to laughter.

with *Thebais* 198-9 and *Oedipus* 855 already quoted.[1] Also IV. 6 :—

> Better I were distract:
> So should my thoughts be sever'd from my griefs;
> And woes, by wrong imaginations lose
> The knowledge of themselves.

> uel sit potius
> mens uaesano concita motu.
> solus te iam praestare potest
> furor insontem.   proxima puris
> sors est manibus nescire nefas.   (*Hercules Furens* 1100-5.)

---

[1] See p. 83.

We tread again on doubtful ground in *Edward III*, although this fine play has been ascribed to Shakspere by very good authorities.[1] In any case, the following comparison is interesting. Act IV.4 :—

>To die is all as common as to live ;
>The one in choice, the other holds in chace :
>For, from the instant we begin to live,
>We do pursue and hunt the time to die :
>First bud we, then we blow, and after seed ;
>Then, presently, we fall ; and, as a shade
>Follows the body, so we follow death.
>If then we hunt for death, why do we fear it?
>If we do fear it, why do we follow it ?
>If we do fear, with fear we do but aid
>The thing we fear to seize on us the sooner :
>If we fear not, then no resolved proffer
>Can overthrow the limit of our fate :
>For, whether ripe or rotten, drop we shall,
>As we do draw the lottery of our doom.

>omnia certo tramite uadunt
>primusque dies dedit extremum.
>non illa deo uertisse licet
>quae nexa suis currunt causis.
>it cuique ratus prece non ulla
>mobilis ordo.
>multis ipsum timuisse nocet.
>multi ad fatum uenere suum
>dum fata timent.   (*Oedipus* 1008-1016.)

Compare also V. 1 :—

>For what the sword cuts down, or fire hath spoiled,
>Is held in reputation none of ours.

---

[1] See Dr. Ward's *History of Dramatic Literature*, I. 456.

with *Thebais* 559-562 :—

> quin tune causae nocet
> ipsum hoc quod armis uertis infestis solum
> segetesque adustas sternis et totos fugam
> edis per agros : nemo sic uastat sua.

Arden of Feversham

In *Arden of Feversham*, another pseudo-Shaksperean tragedy, the following may be noted. Act III. 5 :—

> Well fares the man, howe'er his cates do taste,
> That tables not with foul suspicion ;
> And he but pines amongst his delicates,
> Whose troubled mind is stuff'd with discontent.
> My golden time was when I had no gold ;
> Though then I wanted, then I slept secure ;
> My daily toil begat me night's repose,
> My night's repose made daylight fresh to me :
> But since I climb'd the top bough of the tree,
> And sought to build my nest among the clouds,
> Each gentle stirry gale doth shake my bed,
> And makes me dread my downfall to the earth.

Compare *Hippolytus* 1135-1140 :—

> serunt placidos obscura quies
> praebetque somnos casa securos.
> admota aetheriis culmina sedibus
> duros excipiunt notos
> insani boreae minas
> imbriferumque corum.

Of other plays ascribed to Shakspere, *Locrine* contains many traces of Seneca, both in style and sentiment; but it is a play demanding no special attention, either on account of its date (pr. 1595) or literary merits.

BEN JONSON is said by Theodor Vatke[1] to have specially studied Seneca; but no authority is given for the statement. A comparison between Jonson and Seneca naturally suggests itself from the character of Jonson's genius, and the comparison was made by his contemporaries, both in the commendatory verses prefixed to his works, and in the elegies published after his death under the title of *Jonsonius Virbius*.[2] Seneca finds a place in Jonson's famous lines "to the memory of my beloved master, William Shakspeare," and his name is included in Sir John Daw's miscellaneous list of classical poets (*Epicoene*, II. 2); Jonson gives a number of references to Seneca as notes to *The Masque of Queens*, and in any case he might be safely assumed to have had a close acquaintance with Seneca, for Jonson was thoroughly versed in classical literature, in which, at that period, Seneca held a prominent place. I have been unable, however, to find any statement by Jonson himself that he "specially studied Seneca;" indeed, to judge from the praises of Sophocles and Euripides in the *Discoveries*, and the fact that in the enumeration of Greek and Roman dramatists in the lines to Shakspere the last place is given to "him of Cordova dead" without any special mark of distinction, Jonson was not eager to admit that he followed in the ordinary track by accepting as his model the Roman tragedies which were within easy reach even of those who had "small Latin and less Greek." If this be so, Jonson

---

[1] *Jahrbuch der Deutschen Shakespeare Gesellschaft*, Vol. IV. p. 64.
[2] See Latin lines "In Benjaminum Jonsonum, poetam laureatum, et dramaticorum sui seculi facile principem," and Owen Feltham "To the Memory of Immortal Ben."

owed more to Seneca than he cared to acknowledge, for it was upon Seneca, and not upon the Greek masters, that Jonson modelled his tragic style. In the preface to *Sejanus* he sums up "the offices of a tragic writer" in the phrases "truth of argument, dignity of persons, gravity and height of elocution, fulness and frequency of sentence"—the characteristics, not of Greek tragedy, but of Seneca. He apologises, moreover, for "the want of a proper chorus"—a want which he supplied in *Catiline*, and also in the sketch of *The Fall of Mortimer*, which remained a fragment at his death. Jonson employed the Chorus not after the manner of the Greek, but of the Roman stage, a chorus closing each of the five acts. It is evident, too, that in Jonson's *Catiline*, as in Seneca's tragedies, the Chorus left the stage during the performance of the play, and were supposed to be ignorant of the course of the action, for at the end of Act IV the Chorus profess to be in doubt as to Catiline's designs, which could not have been the case if they had been present when the conspiracy was formed, as would be required by the rules of Greek tragedy. Whalley says in a note to *Catiline:* "Jonson, I think, does not appear to any great advantage in the choruses to this play. My friend Mr. Sympson is also of the same opinion: he says, the sentiments in them are not sufficiently great, nor his measures at all imitative of the ancients; that variety of numbers which runs through all the Greek tragic poets, seems never once to have been his aim. But I imagine Seneca, not Sophocles or Aeschylus, was what he copied after, and 'tis then no wonder that he succeeded no better."

Jonson owed to Seneca something more than the external form of his tragedies; their style and spirit are Roman, not Greek. In striving to attain the "height of elocution" at which he aimed, Jonson is sometimes guilty of Seneca's rhetorical exaggeration of expression; and to this fault he occasionally adds Seneca's physical crudities. The dismemberment of Sejanus is described with a fulness of detail which can only be compared with Seneca's account of the death of Hippolytus; and the speeches of Cethegus in *Catiline* offend in both the ways mentioned, though in this case Jonson justified himself to some extent by making exaggeration and a lust for blood distinctive of the character. Be this as it may, there is an echo of Seneca's style to be discerned in passages like this:—

> It likes me better, that you are not consul.
> I would not go through open doors, but break 'em;
> Swim to my ends through blood; or build a bridge
> Of carcasses; make on upon the heads
> Of men, struck down like piles, to reach the lives
> Of those remain and stand: then is't a prey,
> When danger stops, and ruin makes the way. (III. 1).

In "fulness and frequency of sentence" Jonson assuredly did not fail; but he missed the perfect art of Shakspere, who made his reflections arise naturally from the situation or the character of the speaker. In Jonson, as in Seneca, the "sentences" are introduced with only too obvious design. It should further be remarked that Jonson's indebtedness to Seneca can be traced much more clearly and convincingly than that of Shakspere.

When Shakspere takes a thought suggested by Seneca, it is crystallized in the alembic of his wonder-working imagination, and comes out so changed in form as to bear but slight traces of its origin, so that we are often in doubt whether the thought is not entirely Shakspere's own, and the resemblance to Seneca merely accidental; when Jonson borrows, he takes Seneca's crude ore, and rarely troubles to melt it down and recast it. The following parallels from *Sejanus* may serve as examples:—

I.2:—
                                    Wrath cover'd carries fate:
    Revenge is lost, if I profess my hate.

                ira quae tegitur nocet,
    professa perdunt odia uindictae locum. (*Medea* 153-4.)

II.2—   Thy follies now shall taste what kind of man
    They have provoked, and this thy father's house
    Crack in the flame of my incensed rage,
    Whose fury shall admit no shame or mean.
    Adultery! it is the lightest ill
    I will commit. A race of wicked acts
    Shall flow out of my anger, and o'erspread
    The world's wide face, which no posterity
    Shall e'er approve, nor yet keep silent: things
    That for their cunning, close, and cruel mark,
    Thy father would wish his.

    certetur omni scelere et alterna uice
    stringantur enses. nec sit irarum modus
    pudorue.
    ... ...
    effusus omnis inriget terras cruor
    supraque magnos gentium exultet duces

> libido uictrix. impia stuprum in domo
> leuissimum sit.
> ... ...
> age anime fac quod nulla posteritas probet,
> sed nulla taceat. aliquod audendum est nefas
> atrox cruentum tale quod frater meus
> suum esse malit.   (*Thyestes* 25-7, 44-7, 192-5.)

The dialogue which follows reproduces more or less closely the tyrant's maxims given by Seneca in the *Thyestes*, the *Thebais*, and the *Octavia*. One example will suffice:—

> Whom hatred frights,
> Let him not dream of sovereignty.

> regnare non uult esse qui inuisus timet. (*Thebais* 654.)

And again in the same scene (II. 2) :—

> All modesty is fond: and chiefly where
> The subject is no less compell'd to bear
> Than praise his sovereign's acts.

> maximum hoc regni bonum est,
> quod facta domini cogitur populus sui
> quam ferre tam laudare.   (*Thyestes* 205-7.)

IV. 5 :—   How easily
> Do wretched men believe, what they would have!

> quod nimis miseri uolunt,
> hoc facile credunt.   (*Hercules Furens* 317-8.)

In V. 1 Sejanus says :—

> My roof receives me not; 'tis air I tread;
> And, at each step, I feel my advanced head
> Knock out a star in heaven.

So Atreus in *Thyestes* 888-9 :—

    aequalis astris gradior et cunctos super
    altum superbo uertice attingens polum.

V. 10 :— For, whom the morning saw so great and high,
        Thus low and little 'fore the even doth lie.

    quem dies uidit ueniens superbum,
    hunc dies uidit fugiens iacentem.   (*Thyestes* 613 4.)

It will be noticed above that the *Thyestes* is more frequently laid under contribution than any other play; from the same tragedy Jonson borrowed the opening of *Catiline*, in which the Ghost of Sylla plays the same part as the Ghost of Tantalus in the *Thyestes*; and when the oath of conspiracy is taken, " the day goes back " and murmurings are heard from unseen speakers, " as at Atreus' feast."   Further parallel passages are as under :

[margin: Catiline.]

I.1 :— Behold, I come, sent from the Stygian sound,
        As a dire vapour that had cleft the ground,
        To ingender with the night and blast the day ;
        Or like a pestilence that should display
        Infection through the world.

              mittor ut dirus uapor
    tellure rupta uel grauem populis luem
    sparsura pestis.   (*Thyestes* 87-9.)

    Nor let thy thought find any vacant time
    To hate an old, but still a fresher crime
    Drown the remembrance ; let not mischief cease,
    But while it is in punishing, increase :
    Conscience and care die in thee ; and be free
    Not heaven itself from thy impiety ;

Let night grow blacker with thy plots, and day,
At shewing but thy head forth, start away
From this half-sphere; and leave Rome's blinded walls
To embrace lusts, hatreds, slaughters, funerals.

              nec uacet cuiquam uetus
odisse crimen: semper oriatur nouum
nec unum in uno, dumque punitur scelus,
crescat.
... ...
              fratris et fas et fides
iusque omne pereat. non sit a uestris malis
immune caelum. cum micant stellae polo
seruantque flammae debitum mundo decus,
nox atra fiat, excidat caelo dies.
misce ponates odia caedes funera
arcesse et imple scelere tantaleam domum.
                    (*Thyestes* 29-32, 47-52.)

III. 1 :— Who would not fall with all the world about him?

       uitae est avidus quisquis nonuult
       mundo secum pereunte mori.   (*Thyestes* 886-7.)

III. 2 :— Is there a heaven and gods? and can it be
         They should so slowly hear, so slowly see!
         Hath Jove no thunder?

              magne regnator deum,
       tam lentus audis scelera? tam lentus uides?
       ecquando saeua fulmen emittes manu
       si nunc serenum est?   (*Hippolytus*, 679-682.)

III. 2 :— He that is void of fear, may soon be just.

       iustum esse facile est cui uacat pectus metu.
                    (*Octavia* 453.)

III. 3:—
                    He shall die.
      Shall, was too slowly said ; he's dying : that
      Is yet too slow ; he's dead.

                    si noui Herculem,
      Lycus Creonti debitas poenas dabit.
      lentum est dabit : dat. hoc quoque est lentum : dedit.[1]
                            (*Hercules Furens* 655-7.)

CHAPMAN.

CHAPMAN, like Jonson, seems to have taken Senecan tragedy as his model. In the dedicatory letter prefixed to *The Revenge of Bussy D'Ambois*, he says that "material instruction, elegant and sententious excitation to virtue and deflection from her contrary" are "the soul, limbs, and limits of an authentical tragedy." He is excessively rhetorical, sometimes to the extent of bombast ; he has also Seneca's fault of prolixity ; and he has many elaborate similes such as Seneca occasionally indulged in. Some of these characteristics are no doubt largely accounted for by Chapman's extensive reading in other classical authors, and it must be confessed that his indebtedness to Seneca cannot be clearly proved to any great extent. There are a considerable number of passages suggesting a comparison with Seneca ; but only the following seem to me sufficiently convincing to be worthy of record :—

Byron's Conspiracy III. 1 :—

    LA B. You bid me speak what fear bids me conceal.
    BYR. You have no cause to fear, and therefore speak.

---

[1] These lines have been parodied by Molière in a famous passage of *L'Avare*, IV, 7 :—"Je me meurs, je suis mort, je suis enterré."

LA B. You'll rather wish you had been ignorant,
       Than be instructed in a thing so ill.
BYR.   Ignorance is an idle salve for ill;
       And therefore do not urge me to enforce
       What I would freely know, for by the skill
       Shown in thy aged hairs, I'll lay thy brain
       Here scatter'd at my feet, and seek in that
       What safely thou may'st utter with thy tongue
       If thou deny it.
LA B.   Will you not allow me
       To hold my peace? What less can I desire?
       If not be pleased with my constrained speech.
BYR.   Was ever man yet punished for expressing
       What he was charged? Be free, and speak the worst.

It will be found that all this is taken from *Oedipus* 524-542, except the passage beginning " I'll lay thy brain............," which is a piece of crude bombast worthy of Seneca himself; the same may be said of the speeches of Byron which follow the above extract.

Byron's Conspiracy V. 1 :—

D'AUV.   O my lord,
       This is too large a licence given your fury;
       Give time to it; what reason suddenly
       Cannot extend, respite doth oft supply.

                 da tempus ac spatium tibi.
       quod ratio nequit, saepe sanauit mora.
                              (*Agamemnon* 130-1.)

Byron's Tragedy IV. 1 :—

       Where medicines loathe, it irks men to be heal'd.

       ubi turpis est medicina, sanari piget.   (*Oedipus* 530.)

Byron's Tragedy V. 1 :—

> Why should I keep my soul in this dark light,
> Whose black beams lighted me to lose myself?
> When I have lost my arms, my fame, my mind,
> Friends, brother, hopes, fortunes, and even my fury.

> cur animam in ista luce detineam amplius
> morerque nihil est. cuncta iam amisi bona :
> mentem arma famam coniugem gnatos manus
> etiam furorem.   (*Hercules Furens* 1265-8.)

To the above evidence may be added Chapman's liberal use of sanguinary horrors and ghosts (in *Bussy D'Ambois*, *The Revenge of Bussy D'Ambois*, *Alphonsus Emperor of Germany*, and *Revenge for Honour*), which must be attributed, directly or indirectly, to the example of Seneca.

MARSTON. Of all the Elizabethan dramatists, MARSTON owed the most to Seneca, and was the readiest to acknowledge his indebtedness. He quotes Seneca, both in the Latin[1] and in translation, and from the prose works as well as the tragedies. A quotation from the *Thyestes* finds its way into the preface to *The Fawn*, and in the same comedy we have a line from the *Oedipus* *The Malcontent.* (Mr. Bullen's edition, II. p. 191). In *The Malcontent*, which the author also calls a comedy, Bilioso, essaying to give comfort to Pietro, says, "Marry, I remember one Seneca, Lucius Annaeus Seneca—" and Pietro replies,

---
[1] See Appendix I.

"Out upon him! he writ of temperance and fortitude, yet lived like a voluptuous epicure, and died like an effeminate coward;" again, in Act V. 2, Mendoza says

> Black deed only through black deed safely flies.

and Malevole retorts

> Pooh! *per scelera semper sceleribus tutum est iter.*

the quotation being from *Agamemnon* 116. Notwithstanding these sneers, we have other quotations from Seneca in the same play, both in Latin and English.

> He that can bear with must, he cannot die

in IV. 1 is a translation of Megara's vaunt in *Hercules Furens* 431, "cogi qui potest, nescit mori." From the same source is taken much of Maria's opposition to the suit of Mendoza. Megara says in *Hercules Furens* 423-5:—

> grauent catenae corpus et longa fame
> mors protrahatur lenta. non uincet fidem
> uis ulla nostram. moriar Alcide tua.

So Maria in V. 2:—

> O my dear'st Altofront! where'er thou breathe,
> Let my soul sink into the shades beneath,
> Before I stain thine honour! 'tis thou has't,
> And long as I can die, I will live chaste.

and again in V. 3:—

> Do, urge all torments, all afflictions try;
> I'll die my lords as long as I can die.

In *Hercules Furens* 255-6:—

>   prosperum ac felix scelus
> uirtus uocatur.

we have the original of V.2:—

> Mischief that prospers, men do virtue call.

and the lines that follow,

> Who cannot bear with spite, he cannot rule.
> The chiefest secret for a man of state
> Is, to live senseless of a strengthless hate,

come from *Thebais* 654-6:—

> regnare non uult esse qui inuisus timet.
> simul ista mundi conditor posuit deus
> odium atque regnum.

Antonio and Mellida.   It is, however, in Marston's earlier tragedies, the two parts of *Antonio and Mellida*, that we find the influence of Seneca most plainly manifested, as the following parallels will show.[1] In Part I:—

I. 1:—   'Tis horselike not for man to know his force.

> inertis est nescire quid liceat sibi.   (*Octavia* 465.)

MELL. How covetous thou art of novelties!
Ross. Pish! 'tis our nature to desire things
That are thought strangers to the common cut.

> quisquis secundis rebus exultat nimis
> fluitque luxu semper insolita appetit.[2]
>   (*Hippolytus* 209-210.)

---

[1] One noteworthy passage has already been given. See p. 24.
[2] A slight variation from the Aldine reading.

III. 1 :— Fortune my fortunes, not my mind, shall shake.

fortuna opes auferre non animum potest. (*Medea* 176.)

Alas, survey your fortunes, look what's left
Of all your forces, and your utmost hopes :
A weak old man, a page, and your poor self.

en intuere turba quae simus super :
famulus[1] puer captiua. (*Troas* 516-7.)

No matter whither, but from whence we fall.

magis unde cadas quam quo refert. (*Thyestes* 929.)

IV. 1 :— Give me water, boy.
There is no poison in't, I hope ; they say
That lurks in massy plate.

uenenum in auro bibitur. (*Thyestes* 453.)

AND. Fortune fears valour, presseth cowardice.
LUC. Then valour gets applause, when it hath place,
And means to blaze it.
AND. *Nunquam potest non esse.*
MED. fortuna fortes metuit, ignauos premit.
NVTR. tunc est probanda si locum uirtus habet.
MED. nunquam potest non esse uirtuti locus. (*Medea* 159-161.)

In Part II the borrowing from Seneca is not quite so frequent, but it is still considerable in amount. Mr. Bullen detects "an Attic flavour" in a passage of stichomythia in II. 1, and is momentarily reminded of Creon's altercation with his son in the *Antigone*; as a

---

[1] The Aldine reading is *tumulus*.

matter of fact, the dialogue is borrowed directly and almost entirely from Seneca:—

    PIER. 'Tis just that subjects act commands of kings.
    PAND. Command then just and honourable things.

NERO iussisque nostris pareant.
SEN.   iusta impera.   (*Octavia* 471)

    PIER. Where only honest deeds to kings are free,
           It is no empire, but a beggary.

        ubicumque tantum honesta dominanti licent,
        precario regnatur.   (*Thyestes* 214-5.)

    PIER. Tush, juiceless graybeard, 'tis immunity,
           Proper to princes, that our state exacts;
           Our subjects not alone to bear, but praise our acts.
    PAND. O, but that prince, that worthful praise aspires,
           From hearts, and not from lips, applause desires.
    PIER. Pish!
           True praise the boon of common men doth ring,
           False only girts the temple of a king.

    ATR.   maximum hoc regni bonum est,
        quod facta domini cogitur populus sui
        quam ferre tam laudare.
        ...   .
    SAT. at qui fauoris gloriam ueri petit,
        animo magis quam uoce laudari uolet.
    ATR. laus uera et humili saepe contingit uiro,
        non nisi potenti falsa.   (*Thyestes* 205-7, and 209-212.)

Pandulfo's reply,

    'Tis praise to do, not what we can, but should.

is from *Octavia* 466 :—

id facere laus est quod decet, non quod licet.

The act closes with a quotation from the *Agamemnon*, and the *Thyestes* is laid under contribution once more in the next scene, which is thoroughly Senecan in conception and execution. When the Ghost of Andrea appears again at the opening of Act V, he introduces himself very appropriately by quoting two lines spoken by the shade of Agrippina in the *Octavia*; and the final scene is taken from the *Thyestes*, not only in its main idea, but in the very words of the taunts addressed by Pandulfo to the sinful father who has feasted on his own son. V. 2 :—

He weeps; now do I glorify my hands;
I had no vengeance, if I had no tears.

nunc meas laudo manus,
nunc parta uera est palma. perdideram scelus
nisi sic dolores. (*Thyestes* 1100-2.)

Thy son? true; and which is my most joy,
I hope no bastard, but thy very blood,
Thy true-begotten, most legitimate
And loved issue—there's the comfort on't.

THY. gnatos parenti.
ATR. fáteor et quod me iuuat,
certos. (*Thyestes* 1105-6.)

The rhetorical and reflective style as well as the crude horrors of the two parts of *Antonio and Mellida*, must be ascribed to the influence of Seneca. To Seneca's account, too, we must set down what Mr. Bullen describes as Marston's "besetting fault of straining his style a peg too high; of seeking to be impressive by the use of exaggerated and unnatural imagery." The description of a storm in *The First Part of Antonio and Mellida*, I. 1, which in Mr. Bullen's opinion exhibits this besetting sin of Marston's "to perfection," is modelled on a similar description in Seneca's *Agamemnon*. Compare the opening in each case :—

> The sea grew mad,
> His bowels rumbling with wind-passion;
> Straight swarthy darkness popp'd out Phoebus' eye,
> And blurr'd the jocund face of bright-cheek'd day;
> Whilst crudled fogs masked even darkness' brow :
> Heaven bad's good night, and the rocks groan'd
> At the intestine uproar of the main.

> exigua nubes sordido crescens globo
> nitidum cadentis inquinat Phoebi iubar.
> ... ...
> tractuque longo litus ac petrae gemunt.
> agitata uentis unda uenturis tumet.
> cum luna subito conditur, stellae cadunt,
> in astra pontus tollitur, caelum perit.
> nec una nox est: densa tenebras obruit
> caligo et omni luce subducta fretum
> caelumque miscet.   (*Agamemnon* 483-4 and 489-495.)

and again

> Straight chops a wave, and in in his sliftred paunch
> Down falls our ship, and there he breaks his neck;
> Which in an instant up was belkt again.

> illam dehiscens pontus in praeceps rapit
> hauritque et alto redditam reuomit mare.
>   (*Agamemnon* 520-1.)

But Marston gained something besides unnatural exaggeration from his study of Seneca. Mr. Bullen gives unqualified praise to the "dignified reflections which Marston puts into the mouth of the discrowned Andrugio in the noble speech beginning, 'Why, man, I never was a prince till now.'" This, too, was suggested by Seneca, as will be seen on comparison with *Thyestes* 344-390.

It may be doubted whether Marston ever broke away from the influence of Seneca, though it is certainly less marked in his later plays. Mr. Bullen remarks an improvement in *The Malcontent*, which followed next to *Antonio and Mellida*. "The moralising," he says, "is less tedious, and the satire more pungent than in the earlier plays. There is less of declamation and more of action. The atmosphere is not so stifling, and one can breathe with something of freedom. There are no ghosts to shout 'Vindicta!' and no boys to be butchered at midnight in damp cloisters; nobody has his tongue cut out prior to being hacked to pieces." While one may admit the justice of these observations, it should not be forgotten that *The Malcontent* is described by Marston himself as a comedy. When he returns to tragedy in *Sophonisba*—a tragedy which, he promises, "shall boldly abide the most curious perusal"[1]—he falls back upon Seneca's ghosts and witches, his blood-curdling descriptions of crude horrors decked out with unnatural

---

[1] See the note *To the Reader* prefixed to the second quarto of *The Fawn*.

imagery, his rhetorical artificialities and reflective commonplaces. Much less, however, is borrowed direct from Seneca than in the earlier plays. The description of the habits and abode of the witch Erichtho is taken from Lucan—a writer allied to Seneca not only by close ties of relationship, but by likeness of character, for his genius is essentially philosophic and rhetorical. In the reflective passages, too, of *Sophonisba*, Marston borrowed far less from Seneca than in the earlier plays. The dialogue between Asdrubal and Carthalon at the end of Act II. 3 is quite in Seneca's style, but I have only detected two ideas taken directly from Seneca:—

> He that forbids not offence, he does it.
> qui non uetat peccare, cum possit, iubet.   (*Troas* 300.)

and

> He for whom mischief's done,
> He does it.
>
> cui prodest scelus,
> is fecit.   (*Medea* 503-4.)

The Insatiate Countess is, in Mr. Bullen's opinion, not Marston's, or, at any rate, not all of it. One of the reasons that incline him to this conclusion is the number of passages imitated from Shakspere, among which he includes the following (V. 1):—

> What Tanais, Nilus, or what Tigris swift,
> What Rhenus fierer than the cataract,—
> Although Neptolis cold, the waves of all the Northern Sea,
> Should flow for ever through these guilty hands,
> Yet the sanguinolent stain would extant be!

Mr. Bullen compares this with a well known passage in *Macbeth*, already quoted in this essay.¹ The original of both passages is, I think, to be found in *Hercules Furens* 1330-6:—

> quis Tanais aut quis Nilus aut quis persica
> uiolentus unda Tigris aut Rhenus ferox
> Tagusue hibera turbidus gaza fluens,
> abluere dextram poterit ? arctoum licet
> Maeotis in me gelida transfundat mare
> et tota Tethys per meas currat manus:
> haerebit altum facinus.

From the closeness of the translation in *The Insatiate Countess*, it is evident that the author borrowed from Seneca direct; and it seems to me that the reading "Neptolis," for which Mr. Bullen suggests the emendation "Neptune," might safely be altered to the "Maeotis" of the original. Moreover, this passage, imitated not from Shakspere but from Seneca, testifies in favour of Marston's authorship, and not, as Mr. Bullen thinks, against it.

In the same school as Marston's *Antonio and Mellida* must be included CHETTLE's *Hoffman; or a Revenge for a Father*, which was not printed till 1631, but (as we learn from Henslowe's *Diary*) was written in 1602. The tragedy opens before a cave at the entrance of which there is "a skeleton hanging on a tree in chains, with an iron crown on its head." Amid thunder and lightning Hoffman addresses his murdered father's skeleton, "which rattles

---
¹ See p. 84.

from the wind in its chains." Then appears the first victim of Hoffman's revenge, Prince Otho, who is bound to the rock and tortured to death (on the stage) with the iron crown, which has been taken from the head of the skeleton, and made red hot. Hoffman, having stripped the flesh off the bones, hangs the skeleton in chains, by the side of that of his father, upon the tree, and speaks thus :—

> Come, image of bare death, join side to side
> With my long-injur'd father's naked bones!
> He was the prologue to a tragedy,
> That, if my destinies deny me not,
> Shall pass those of Thyestes, Tereus,
> Jocasta, or Duke Jason's jealous wife.

The "dismal accidents and bloody deeds, poisonings and treasons" which follow bid fair to fulfil the promise that Seneca's gruesome themes shall be outdone. In the end, Hoffman is bound to the rock, and tortured with the iron crown, made red hot; this alone prevents him from adding rape to a succession of murders, and he dies regretting that he has

> slackt revenge
> Through fickle beauty and a woman's fraud.

There are occasional reflective passages in Seneca's style, and some reminiscences of his ideas, but they are neither striking nor important. There is a close resemblance throughout to Seneca's mode of treating his bloody themes, Act IV. 3 giving a noteworthy example of the rhetorical and amplified horror which we have remarked as one of Seneca's most striking characteristics. Take for instance the passage :—

> Thou wert as good, and better, (note my words)
> Run unto the top of [some] dreadful scar
> And thence fall headlong on the under rocks;
> Or set thy breast against a cannon fir'd,
> When iron death flies thence on flaming wings;
> Or with thy shoulders, Atlas-like, attempt
> To bear the ruins of a falling tower;
> Or swim the ocean, or run quick to hell,
> (As dead assure thyself no better place)
> Than once look frowning on this angel's face.

Seneca's fondness for these exaggerated comparisons has been already noted.[1]

Lust's Dominion (pr. 1657), a tragedy of similar character to the preceding, but of more inept workmanship, is only of importance on account of its supposed identity with DEKKER's *Spanish Moor's Tragedy*, acted in January, 1599-1600. It contains bombast in abundance, and sententious reflections in Seneca's manner, sometimes with an echo of his ideas.

Lust's Dominion: DEKKER!

WEBSTER and TOURNEUR further developed the Tragedy of Blood (as Mr. Symonds calls it), which by their time had been long familiar to English

WEBSTER and TOURNEUR.

---
[1] See page 19.

audiences and readers; and the indirect influence of Seneca acting through their predecessors in English tragedy had probably more effect upon them than any first-hand study of the Roman dramatist, of which we have little evidence. In *The Revenger's Tragedy* Tourneur misquotes a single line from Seneca—the familiar

> curae leues loquuntur ingentes stupent.[1]

The same thought is reproduced by Webster in *The White Devil*, II. 1: —

> Unkindness, do thy office; poor heart, break:
> Those are the killing griefs which dare not speak.

but it seems likely that this was a reminiscence of Shakspere, and was not taken directly from Seneca. The same may be said of another line in the same scene:—

> Small mischiefs are by greater made secure.

Another idea common to Shakspere and Seneca is reproduced by Tourneur in *The Revenger's Tragedy*, V. 3:—

> He that climbs highest has the greatest fall.

A passage in the same play II. 4:—

> It well becomes that judge to nod at crimes
> That does commit greater himself, and lives.

may be compared with *Agamemnon* 268:—

> det ille ueniam facile cui uenia est opus.

---

[1] See Appendix I.

Tourneur has also effectively developed an idea suggested in *Hippolytus* 679-682 :—

>   magne regnator deum
>   tam lentus audis scelera? tam lentus uides?
>   ecquando saeua fulmen emittes manu
>   si nunc serenum est?

In *The Revenger's Tragedy*, IV. 2 Vendice says:—

> O thou almighty patience! 'tis my wonder
> That such a fellow, impudent and wicked,
> Should not be cloven as he stood;
> Or with a secret wind burst open!
> Is there no thunder left; or is't kept up
> In stock for heavier vengeance? [*Thunder*] there it goes!

The same device is employed once more in the last scene.

More striking, however, than the resemblance of isolated passages is the resemblance in theme and mode of treatment. Webster and Tourneur, like Seneca, choose themes of lust, murder, incest, and unnatural crime; they employ the same devices of ghosts and the ghastly relics of mortality; their tragedies breathe the same atmosphere of blood. By the side of these heaped up horrors, which Webster depicted with unique dramatic power and psychological insight, we have something of Seneca's reflective tendency, and occasionally a likeness in the thoughts expressed, as may be remarked in the the passages quoted above. We have Seneca's fatalism in *The Duchess of Malfi*, V. 4 :—

> We are merely the stars' tennis balls, struck and bandied
> Which way please them.

and Seneca's Stoicism in V. 3 of the same play:—

> Though in our miseries Fortune have a part,
> Yet in our noble sufferings she hath none:
> Contempt of pain, that we may call our own.

Tourneur amplifies the same idea in *The Atheist's Tragedy*, III. 3, in Charlemont's defiance of Sebastian and his father. To the same source we may ascribe the Stoical calmness with which the characters of both dramatists meet death. See, for instance, the last speech of the Duchess of Malfi; Vittoria Corrombona welcomes death "as princes do some great ambassador;" she meets the weapon half-way, and sheds "not one base tear." Flamineo, her villainous brother, ends his life with a laugh, and the reflection,

> We cease to grieve, cease to be fortune's slaves,
> Nay, cease to die, by dying.

Bosola, the villain of *The Duchess of Malfi*, dies with hardly less constancy. Charlemont and Castabella in *The Atheist's Tragedy* seek death with equal hardihood; and in *The Revenger's Tragedy* Vendice accepts death for himself as calmly as he dealt it out to others.

FORD. Ford abounds in his own kind of tragic horrors, and he is not altogether free from crude sensationalism; in *'Tis Pity She's a Whore*, Giovanni enters with his sister's heart upon his dagger, and Ford's plays generally treat of such "strong" themes as incest, adultery, and murderous revenge. But the atmosphere of his tragedies does not overpower us with the smell of blood, as in the case of Webster and Tourneur; there is often a fresher, purer air of quiet thought and natural passion. Ford makes little use of the supernatural; in all probability Mother Sawyer and her familiars in *The Witch of Edmonton* are the creations of Dekker, and the only spirit to be set down to Ford's account is the quiet and inoffensive ghost of Susan, which comes to the bedside of her husband and murderer, and stands there without saying a word. Ford's genius was of too refined a character to seek the strong and coarse effects which were achieved by some of his contemporaries and predecessors. Occasionally he is guilty of rhetorical exaggeration, as in *The Broken Heart*, IV. 1:—

> In anger!
> In anger let him part; for could his breath,
> Like whirlwinds, toss such servile slaves as lick
> The dust his footsteps print into a vapour,
> It durst not stir a hair of mine, it should not;
> I'd rend it up by the roots first.

And again in *Love's Sacrifice*, IV. 2:—

> I have a sword—'tis here—should make my way
> Through fire, through darkness, death, and hell, and all,
> To hew your lust-engendered flesh to shreds,
> Pound you to mortar, cut your throats, and mince
> Your flesh to mites: I will,—start not,—I will.

But extravagance is pardonable in the mouths of characters like Ithocles and the Duke in their respective situations.

In Ford the reflective tendency is strongly marked, but his manner is all his own. He had a marvellous gift for expressing deep and yet simple thought, far removed from Seneca's artificial and strained dialectic, which was probably its far-back ancestor. Nothing could show the contrast better than the comparison of Seneca's well-worn maxim,

> curae leues loquuntur ingentes stupent,

with the magnificent passage in which Ford enlarges on the same idea. *The Broken Heart*, V. 3 :—

> O, my lords,
> I but deceived your eyes with antic gesture,
> When one news straight came huddling on another
> Of death! and death! and death! still I danced forward;
> But it struck home, and here, and in an instant.
> Be such mere women, who with shrieks and outcries
> Can vow a present end to all their sorrows,
> Yet live to court new pleasures, and outlive them:
> They are the silent griefs which cut the heart-strings;
> Let me die smiling.

Probably the points in which Ford drew nearest to Seneca and in which he owes most to him (if indeed he owes anything at all) are those previously remarked in the case of his contemporaries. Ford, like Seneca, was a fatalist. Thus Orgilus in *The Broken Heart*, I. 3 :—

> Ingenious Fate has leapt into mine arms,
> Beyond the compass of my brain. Mortality
> Creeps on the dung of earth, and cannot reach
> The riddles which are purposed by the gods,

The same thought closes Act IV of *Love's Sacrifice*, and occurs again and again in the domestic tragedy of *The Witch of Edmonton*, the only part of that drama we should ascribe to Ford. With this fatalism is allied the idea of Stoical submission. Thus Lady Katherine in *Perkin Warbeck*, III. 2 :—

> What our destinies
> Have ruled out in their books we must not search,
> But kneel to.

So, too, Ithocles in *The Broken Heart*, IV. 1:—

> Leave to the powers
> Above us the effects of their decrees;
> My burthen lies within me: servile fears
> Prevent no great effects.

To the influence of Seneca, direct or indirect, we should probably ascribe the calmness with which Ford's characters meet death. Perkin Warbeck closes his life with the words,

> Death? pish! 'tis but a sound; a name of air... ...

The innocent Susan in *The Witch of Edmonton*; the guilty brother and sister in *'Tis Pity She's a Whore*; Ithocles, Orgilus, and Calantha in *The Broken Heart*; Bianca, Fernando, and the Duke in *Love's Sacrifice*—all are alike in their contempt for death; they rather seek it than fear it.

BEAUMONT and FLETCHER.

BEAUMONT and FLETCHER, in *The Knight of the Burning Pestle*, made fun of the philosophical commonplaces,[1] the bombast, and the supernatural horrors which dramatists like Marston borrowed from Seneca; but Beaumont and Fletcher are themselves not free from occasional exaggeration of expression;[2] ghosts or spirits appear in several of the plays in which Fletcher had a hand,[3] and in one or two the tragic effect is of a somewhat gruesome character. Thus in *The Triumph of Death* (probably by Fletcher alone), amid the wholesale slaughter which closes the play, Gabriella tears out her husband's heart, and throws it at his uncle's feet; and in *The Bloody Brother* (by Fletcher and Massinger), the heads of Gisbert and Hamond are brought on the stage after their execution. Still, it must be acknowledged that Fletcher and his chief co-adjutors, Beaumont and Massinger, owe little to Seneca. Their most important debt was probably the Stoical fortitude with which their characters are inspired in face of death. Fletcher has sometimes been credited with weakness in this respect;[4] but, so far as I can see, it is little less remarkable in the plays which Fletcher wrote alone than in

---

[1] Ralph's reflection, (V. 2), "To a resolved mind his home is every where," is evidently a parody of *Antonio and Mellida*, 2nd Part, II. 1, "A wise man's home is wheresoe'er he is wise"—a maxim which Marston borrowed from Seneca.

[2] See *Philaster*, III.1. "Set hills on hills..." and IV. 4. "Place me, some god, upon a pyramis......;" speeches of Arbaces in *A King and no King*; and Fletcher's *A Wife for a Month*, IV.4.

[3] In *The Lover's Progress* and *The Prophetess*, by Fletcher and Massinger, and in *The Humorous Lieutenant* and *The Triumph of Death*, by Fletcher alone.

[4] See Mr. R. Boyle's note on *Barnavelt*.

those written in conjunction with others. In Fletcher's *Valentinian*, IV. 4, Aecius says:—

> We must all die,
> All leave ourselves; it matters not where, when,
> Nor how, so we die well.

So too Young Archas in I. 4 of *The Loyal Subject*, another play written by Fletcher alone:—

> 'Tis but dying,
> And, madam, we must do it; the manner's all.

and his father in IV. 5 :—

> I am the same, the same man, living, dying;
> The same mind to 'em both, I poize thus equal.

See also the deaths of Bonduca and her daughters in Fletcher's tragedy, for, as in Seneca, the women are no less brave than the men. We note this as well in the work which Fletcher did in co-operation with Beaumont as in the later tragedies in which he had the assistance of Massinger. When Philaster (III. 1) says to the disguised Euphrasia,

> Oh, but thou dost not know
> What 'tis to die.

she replies

> Yes, I do know, my lord:
> 'Tis less than to be born; a lasting sleep;
> A quiet resting from all jealousy,
> A thing we all pursue; I know, besides,
> It is but giving over of a game
> That must be lost.

and Ordella in Fletcher and Massinger's *Thierry and Theodoret* says,

> 'Tis of all sleeps the sweetest:
> Children begin it to us, strong men seek it,
> And kings from height of all their painted glories
> Fall like spent exhalations to this centre:
> And those are fools that fear it.

In *The Double Marriage*, another play by Fletcher and Massinger, Juliana is as heroic in her contempt for death as her husband, and Martia as unflinching as her valiant father.

Reflective passages in the plays passing under the names of Beaumont and Fletcher are not numerous, and though in some cases the thought expressed may be interpreted as a reminiscence of Seneca, there are few instances in which the resemblance is not just as likely to be merely accidental. Thus, Philaster's exclamation (III. 1. *ad fin.*)

> Oh, where shall I
> Go bathe this body? Nature too unkind,
> That made no medicine for a troubled mind!

may be compared with *Hercules Furens* 1330-6, "Quis Tanais........" and 1268-9, "Nemo polluto queat animo mederi;" but it seems useless to multiply parallels of this kind. The only example I have found of direct imitation is in the scene between Sophia and her two sons in *The Bloody Brother* (I. 1), which is largely borrowed from Seneca, as the following extracts will show:—

The Bloody Brother

on *Elizabethan Tragedy.* 119

SOPH. And join your hands while they are innocent!
You have heat of blood, and youth apt to ambition,
To plead an easy pardon for what's past;
But all the ills beyond this hour committed,
From gods or men must hope for no excuse.

    dexteras matri date.
date dum piae sunt. error inuitos adhuc
fecit nocentes, omne fortunae fuit
peccantis in uos crimen : hoc primum nefas
inter scientes geritur.   (*Thebais* 450-4.)

and again

    Why dost thou tremble,
And with a fearful eye, fix'd on thy brother,
Observ'st his ready sword, as bent against thee?
I am thy armour, and will be pierc'd through
Ten thousand times, before I will give way
To any peril may arrive at thee ;
And therefore fear not.

    quo uultus refers
acieque pauida fratris obseruas manum?
adfusa totum corpus amplexu tegam
tuo cruori per meum fiet uia.
quid dubius haeres? an times matris fidem?
      (*Thebais* 473-7.)

SOPH. (*returning the sword*)
Take it again, and stand upon your guard,
And, while your brother is, continue arm'd.

    redde iam capulo manum,
adstringe galeam, laeua se clipeo ingerat,
dum frater est armatus, armatus mane. (*Thebais* 480-2.)

You doubt him; he fears you; I doubt and fear
Both, for [the] other's safety, not my own.
Know yet, my sons, when of necessity
You must deceive or be deceiv'd, 'tis better
To suffer treason than to act the traitor;
And in a war like this, in which the glory
Is his that's overcome. Consider, then,
What 'tis for which you strive: is it the dukedom?
Or the command of these so ready subjects?
Desire of wealth? or whatsoever else
Fires your ambition? 'tis still desperate madness,
To kill the people which you would be lords of;
With fire and sword to lay that country waste
Whose rule you seek for; to consume the treasures,
Which are the sinews of your government,
In cherishing the factions that destroy it:
Far, far be this from you! make it not question'd
Whether you can have interest in that dukedom
Whose ruin both contend for.

                    ille te tu illum times,
ego utrumque, sed pro utroque...   ...   ...
id gerere bellum cupitis in quo est optimum
uinci. uereris fratris infesti dolos?
quotiens necesse est fallere aut falli a suis,
patiare potius ipse quam facias scelus.
...   .
                  quis tenet mentem furor?
petendo patriam perdis? ut fiat tua,
uis esse nullam? quin tuae causae nocet
ipsum hoc quod armis uertis infestis solum
segetesque adustas sternis et totos fugam
edis per agros: nemo sic uastat sua.
quae corripi igne quae meti gladio iubes
aliena credis? rex sit e uobis uter
manente regno quaerite.   (*Thebais* 488-494, 557-565.)

It should be noted that Mr. Oliphant, Mr. Boyle, MASSINGER. and Mr. Bullen agree in ascribing the above passage to MASSINGER, who is more nearly allied to Seneca than Beaumont and Fletcher, his genius being, as Dr. Ward remarks, "essentially rhetorical." He is not entirely free from bombast,[1] and in some of his plays he relies for dramatic effect upon the physical horrors which we have remarked as the chief characteristic of the English school of Seneca. Nothing could be more repulsive than the outrage done to the dead body of Marcelia in *The Duke of Milan*; and the theme of *The Unnatural Combat* is bloody and horrible enough. The conclusion of the latter drama is brought about in a manner worthy of the most devoted imitator of Seneca's ghosts and crude horrors, the stage direction reading:— "Enter the Ghost of young Malefort, naked from the waist, full of wounds, leading in the Shadow of a Lady, her face leprous." Seneca is mentioned two or three times in different plays,[2] and I have noted one or two parallels in addition to the extract from *The Bloody Brother* quoted above; but they are not very striking. The following passages express ideas derived from Seneca, but by Massinger's time long familiar to the English drama. *The Duke of Milan*, I. 3 :—

<blockquote>
The only blessing that
Heaven hath bestowed on us, more than on beasts,
</blockquote>

---

[1] *e. g.* Sforza in *The Duke of Milan*, V. 2; Slave in *The Virgin Martyr*, IV. 1.
[2] *The Maid of Honour*, IV. 3; *The Roman Actor*, III. 2.

> Is, that 'tis in our pleasure when to die.
> Besides, were I now in another's power,
> There are so many ways to let out life,
> I would not live, for one short minute, his ;
> I was born only yours, and I will die so.

The Bashful Lover, IV. 1 :—

> HORT. Virtue's but a word ;
>   Fortune rules all.
> MAT. We are her tennis balls.

Massinger is not, however, a thorough-going fatalist like Ford, Webster, and Tourneur. His general attitude is more correctly represented by the concluding speech of Lorenzo in the play just quoted :—

>   Fortune here hath shown
> Her various power; but virtue, in the end,
> Is crown'd with laurel.

Another mark of the influence of Seneca is to be found less clearly in Massinger than in some of his contemporaries—the steadfastness with which the characters meet death. This is not so characteristic of Massinger as of the Seneca school proper; but instances of it are not wanting. The converts in *The Christian Martyr* of course meet death with Christian fortitude; and the calmness of Antiochus in *Believe as you List* is nothing more than we should expect from his royal character and Stoical training. It is more to the point to note that Francisco, the villain in *The Duke of Milan*, meets death undaunted; and see also the beautiful song with which Eudocia in *The Emperor of the East*, V. 3 welcomes " the long and quiet sleep of death."

SHIRLEY, the last of the giant race, marks the emancipation of English tragedy from the authority of Seneca, except so far as regards the character of his themes. The subjects of his tragedies are still themes of lust and blood, and it would be hard to find a more striking example of heaped-up horrors than the conclusion of *The Traitor*. Still, as Mr. Dyce remarks, " in only one of his plays, *St. Patrick for Ireland*, is supernatural agency employed; and in not one of them does a ghost make its appearance." Again, Seneca's philosophy had little or no effect upon Shirley. He was not a fatalist, and his characters are far from Stoical. His most determined hero, Sciarrha, says, in *The Traitor*, IV. 2:—

> Although I never fear'd to suffer, I
> Am not so foolish to despise a life.

—a very different sentiment to the eagerness for death represented by the followers of Seneca. The Cardinal, again, ends his wicked life with the despairing cry:—

> If you but waft me with a little prayer;
> My wings that flag might catch the wind; but 'tis
> In vain, the mist is risen, and there's none
> To steer my wandering bark.

—a striking contrast to the fearlessness in face of death

shown by the desperate villains of Webster, whose style Shirley is thought to have imitated in *The Cardinal*.

Conclusion.   With Shirley our survey of the drama closes. We might go further, and inquire into the influence Seneca had, at first or second hand, upon Milton's conception of tragedy ; we might attempt to estimate Dryden's indebtedness to Seneca, and examine the imitations or adaptations of Seneca by Crowne, Thomson, and Glover. The influence of Seneca was paramount in English tragedy till far into the eighteenth century. It is little more than a hundred years since Greek literature began to exert a broad and steady influence on our poetry. Professor J. W. Hales observes in an article on "The Last Decade of the Last Century" in the current[1] number of the *Contemporary Review* that "the critics and authors of the eighteenth century are for ever talking about the classics ; but, if we observe their remarks, we shall find for the most part that they mean the Latin classics—that they have little or no real acquaintance with the Greek. .... If we take a glance at the classical tragedies that were in esteem, we find they belong to the school of Seneca rather than that of Sophocles." But it does not seem worth while to prove this by detailed examination. The importance of Seneca's influence on the drama is at an end, and it only remains for us to sum up its abiding results, which we find chiefly in the stage traditions which have come down to our own day.

---

[1] **September, 1892.**

Seneca's five acts are still with us, and we have a curious survival from the classical drama in the operatic chorus. Our conception of tragedy still leads us to expect deeds of violence and blood, vividly presented in highly wrought scenes, and weighted with well-expressed thought. Mr. Symonds seems to me to undervalue the reflective element which the authority of Seneca induced in Elizabethan tragedy. He is inclined to lay it down as a principle that "in proportion as a dramatist lends himself to the compilation of ethical anthologies, in that very measure he is an inferior master of his craft." Seeing that an industrious compiler has found no less than 2,700 "mottoes and aphorisms" in Shakspere, Mr. Symonds' standard, if rigidly applied, would seem to endanger the fame of the greatest of the Elizabethans; and such a result is enough to call for a revision of the standard of judgement. In his *Guide to Greek Tragedy*, Dr. Campbell has some admirable remarks showing that the element of ethical reflection "enters almost necessarily into all tragedy;" he says further that all great tragedy is at once individual and universal. Seneca often loses sight of the individual in the universal; but the tendency of the popular drama in England would have been in the opposite direction, and in correcting this tendency Seneca seems to me to have done good service to the Elizabethan drama, giving it permanent value, for the study as well as for the stage. That Seneca misled English dramatists into violence and exaggeration cannot be denied; but these are faults which have their favourable side. If Elizabethan tragedy is sometimes too sensational, it is very seldom dull; and if its diction is sometimes extravagant, it is rarely inadequate to the needs of the situation, however tremendous the tragic crisis may be. What English tragedy would have been without the example of Seneca, it is hard to imagine; its developement from the miracle plays and moralities must have been exceedingly slow; and if the impulse had come from other European nations, it would only have been the influence of Seneca at second hand, in the case of France with exaggerated artificiality, in the case of Italy with exaggerated horrors. Even the direct imitation of Greek tragedy, in all the perfection of Sophocles, might not have been an unmixed blessing; but, after all, literary criticism is concerned, not with what might have been, but with what was; and that the influence of Seneca was paramount in the origin and developement of Elizabethan tragedy has been proved by the testimony of contemporary critics, and by the still more convincing evidence of the tragedies themselves.

APPENDIX I.

Latin Quotations from Seneca in Elizabethan Tragedies.

SIR THOMAS MORE.

Ubi turpis est medicina, sanari piget. (*Oedipus* 530.)
Humida vallis raros patitur fulminis ictus. (*Hippolytus* 1141-2.)
Curae leues loquuntur, ingentes stupent. (*Hippolytus* 615.)

 The last quotation also occurs in *The Return from Parnassus*, and in TOURNEUR'S *Revenger's Tragedy*, *majores* being inserted in the latter case instead of the correct reading *ingentes*.

THE TRUE TRAGEDY OF RICHARD III.

Quisquam regna gaudit, ô fallex bonum.
[quisquamne regno gaudet? o fallax bonum. (*Oedipus* 6.)]

KYD'S SPANISH TRAGEDY.

Per scelus semper tutum est sceleribus iter.
[per scelera semper sceleribus tutum est iter. (*Agamemnon* 116.)]

Fata si miseros juvant, habes salutem ;
Fata si vitam negant, habes sepulchrum. (*Troas* 518-520.)

MARLOWE'S EDWARD II.

Quem dies vidit veniens superbum,
Hunc dies vidit fugiens jacentem.   (*Thyestes* 613-4.)

TITUS ANDRONICUS.

Sit fas aut nefas... ... ...
Per Styga, per manes vehor.

[et te per undas perque tartareos lacus
per Styga per amnes igneos amens sequar. (*Hippolytus* 1188-9.)]

Magni Dominator poli,
Tam lentus audis scelera? tam lentus vides?

            [magne regnator deum,
tam lentus audis scelera? tam lentus uides? (*Hippolytus* 679-80.)]

MARSTON'S ANTONIO AND MELLIDA.

Dimitto superos, summa votorum attigi. (*Thyestes* 891.)

Capienda rebus in malis praeceps via est. (*Agamemnon* 155.)

Scelera non ulcisceris, nisi vincis. (*Thyestes* 195-6.)

       O quisquis nova
Supplicia functis dirus umbrarum arbiter
Disponis, quisquis exeso jaces
Pavidus sub antro, quisquis venturi times
Montis ruinam, quisquis avidorum feros
Rictus leonum, et dira furiarum agmina
Implicitus horres, Antonii vocem excipe
Properantis ad vos.

[*Thyestes* 13-15 and 75-81 run together, with *Antonii* put instead of *Tantali*.]

Venit in nostras manus
Taudem vindicta, venit et tota quidem. (*Thyestes* 494-5.)

[*Vindicta............tota = Thyestes........... totus* in Seneca.]

Venit dies, tempusque, quo reddat suis
Animam squalentem sceleribus. (*Octavia* 641-2.)

[*Venit = veniet, squalentem = nocentem.*]

THE MALCONTENT.

Unde cadis, non quo, refert.

[magis unde cadas quam quo refert. (*Thyestes* 929.)]

Praemium incertum petit certum scelus. (*Thebais* 632-3.)

Per scelera semper sceleribus tutum est iter. (*Agamemnon* 116.)

THE FAWN.

Qui nimis notus omnibus
Ignotus moritur sibi. (*Thyestes* 402-3.)

Fatis agimur, cedite fatis. (*Oedipus* 1001.)

APPENDIX II.

Imitations of Seneca
IN
THE MISFORTUNES OF ARTHUR.

The pages refer to Vol. IV of Hazlitt's *Dodsley*. There are 37 lines in a full page, which will give the reader some idea of the proportion of borrowed lines. In some cases half or more than half the page is borrowed.[1] Besides the passages given, there are many which seem to have been suggested by Seneca; but I have only thought those worthy of record in which the imitation is obvious.

>Page 264. Let mischiefs know no mean, nor plagues an end!
>Let th' offspring's sin exceed the former stock!
>Let none have time to hate his former fault,
>But still with fresh supply let punish'd crime
>Increase, till time it make a complete sin.
>
>   nec sit irarum modus
>pudorue: mentes caecus instiget furor,
>rabies parentum duret et longum nefas
>eat in nepotes. nec uacet cuiquam uetus
>odisse crimen: semper oriatur nouum
>nec unum in uno, dumque punitur scelus,
>crescat.   (*Thyestes* 26-32.)

---

[1] On page 266 there are not half a dozen original lines.

Page 264   Go to : some fact, which no age shall allow
(continued).   Nor yet conceal—

> age anime fac quod nulla posteritas probet,
> sed nulla taceat.   (*Thyestes* 192-3.)

Page 265.   Attempt some bloody, dreadful, irksome fact,
And such as Mordred would were rather his.

> aliquod audendum est nefas
> atrox cruentum tale quod frater meus
> suum esse malit.   (*Thyestes* 193-5.)

Page 266.   Frame out some trap beyond all vulgar guile,
Beyond Medea's wiles: attempt some fact,
That any wight unwieldy of herself,
That any spouse unfaithful to her pheer,
Durst e'er attempt in most despair of weal.
Spare no revenge, b' it poison, knife, or fire !

> tecum ipsa nunc euolue femineos dolos,
> quod ulla coniunx perfida atque impos sui
> amore caeco, quod nouercales manus
> ausae, quod ardens impia uirgo face
> phasiaca fugiens regna thessalica trabe :
> ferrum uenena.   (*Agamemnon* 117-122.)

,,   The wrath that breatheth blood doth loathe to lurk.

> cum spirat ira sanguinem nescit tegi.   (*Thyestes* 504.)

,,   I am disdain'd : so will I not be long.
That very hour that he shall first arrive,
Shall be the last that shall afford him life.

> iam displicemus, capta praelata est mihi.
> non praeferetur : qui dies thalami ultimus
> nostri est futurus, hic erit uitae tuae.
>   (*Hercules Octaeus* 307-9.)

Page 266
(continued).

Though neither seas, nor lands, nor wars abroad
Sufficed for thy foil, yet shalt thou find
Far worse at home—thy deep-displeased spouse.
Whate'er thou hast subdued in all thy stay
This hand shall now subdue.

          gesseris caelum licet
totusque pacem debeat mundus tibi:
est aliquid hydra peius iratae dolor
nuptae. quis ignis tantus in caelum furit
ardentis Aetnae? quicquid est uictum tibi
hic uincet animus.   (*Hercules Oetaeus* 285-290.)

"   What's this? my mind recoils and irks these threats:
Anger delays, my grief gins to assuage,
My fury faints, and sacred wedlock's faith
Presents itself. Why shunn'st thou fearful wrath?
Add coals afresh: preserve me to this venge.

quid hoc? recedit animus et ponit minas,
iam cessit ira. quid miser langues dolor?
perdis furorem, coniugis sanctae fidem
mihi reddis iterum. quid uetas flammas ali?
quid frangis ignes? hunc mihi serua impetum.
                    (*Hercules Oetaeus* 310-314.)

"   At least exile thyself to realms unknown,
And steal his wealth to help thy banish'd state;
For flight is best. O base and heartless fear!
Theft? Exile? Flight? all these may fortune send
Unsought; but thee beseems more high revenge.

          uel mycenaea domo
coniuncta socio profuge furtiua rate.
quid timida loqueris furta et exilium et fugas?
sors ista fecit. te decet maius nefas.
                    (*Agamemnon* 122-5.)

Page 266 Come, spiteful fiends, come, heaps of furies fell,
(continued). Not one by one, but all at once! my breast
Page 267. Raves not enough: it likes me to be fill'd
With greater monsters yet.

      dira furiarum cohors
discorsque Erinnys ueniat et geminas faces
Megaera quatiens. non satis magno meum
ardet furore pectus, impleri iuuat
maiore monstro.   (*Thyestes* 250-254.)

„   My heart doth throb,
My liver boils: somewhat my mind portends,
Uncertain what; but whatsoever, it's huge.

nescio quid animus maius et solito amplius
supraque fines moris humani tumet
instatque pigris manibus. haud quid sit scio,
sed grande quiddam est.   (*Thyestes* 267-270.)

„ Omit no plague, and none will be enough.

nullum relinquam facinus et nullum est satis.
          (*Thyestes* 256.)

„ Wrong cannot be reveng'd but by excess.

     scelera non ulcisceris
nisi uincis.   (*Thyestes* 195-6.)

„ FRON.   Is there no mean in wrong?
  GUEN. Wrong claims a mean, when first you offer wrong:
    The mean is vain when wrong is in revenge.

  THY.   sceleris est aliquis modus.
  ATR. sceleri modus debetur, ubi facias scelus,
    non ubi reponas.   (*Thyestes* 1055-7.)

Page 267   Great harms cannot be hid : the grief is small,
(continued).   That can receive advice, or rule itself.

        leuis est dolor qui capere consilium potest
        et clepere sese, magna non latitant mala.   (*Medea* 155-6.)

   „   Hatred conceal'd doth often lap to hurt,
       But once profess'd, it oft'ner fails revenge.

                ira quae tegitur nocet,
        professa perdunt odia uindictae locum.   (*Medea* 153-4.)

   „   Unlawful love doth like, when lawful loathes.

        inlicita amantur, excidit quicquid licet.
                                     (*Hercules Oetaeus* 360.)

Page 268.   Fron.   How can you then attempt a fresh offence ?
            Guen.   Who can appoint a stint to her offence ?

            Nvt.   piget prioris et nouum crimen struis ?
            Cly.   res est profecto stulta nequitiae modus.
                                 (*Agamemnon* 150-151.)

   „   Whom Gods do press, they bend ; whom man annoys,
       He breaks.

        caelestis ira quos premit, miseros facit,
        humana nullos.   (*Hercules Oetaeus* 444-5.)

   „   Your grief is more than his deserts.
       Each fault requires an equal hate : be not severe,
       Where crimes be light.   As you have felt, so grieve.

                      maior admisso tuus
        alumna dolor est : culpa par odium exigat.
        cur saeua modice statuis ? ut passa es dole.
                               (*Hercules Oetaeus* 447-9.)

Page 269. Well, shame is not so quite exil'd, but that
I can and will respect your sage advice.

    non omnis animo cessit ingenuo pudor :
    paremus altrix.   (*Hippolytus* 255-6.)

,,   The love, that for his rage will not be rul'd,
Must be restrain'd : fame shall receive no foil.

            qui regi non uvlt amor
    uincatur.   haud te fama maculari sinam.
                                  (*Hippolytus* 256-7.)

,,   Her breast, not yet appeas'd from former rage,
Hath chang'd her wrath which, wanting means to work
Another's woe (for such is fury's wont),
Seeks out his own, and raves upon itself.

    nondum tumultu pectus attonitum caret
    mutauit iras quodque habet proprium furor,
    in se ipse saeuit.   (*Hercules Furens* 1226-8.)

,,   Thereby the rather you deserve to live
For seeming worthy in yourself to die.

            dignam ob hoc uita reor
    quod esse temet autumas dignam nece. (*Hippolytus* 261-2.)

,,
Page 270.   Death is decreed, what kind of death, I doubt :
Whether to drown or stifle up this breath,
Or forcing blood to die with dint of knife.

    decreta mors est : quaeritur fati genus.
    laqueone uitam finiam an ferro incubem ?
                                (*Hippolytus* 263-4.)

Page 270 All hope of prosperous hap is gone.. My fame,
(continued). My'faith, my spouse—no good is left unlost!

    cuncta iam amisi bona:
  montem arma famam coniugem. (*Hercules Furens* 1266-7.)

,, Myself am left: there's left both seas and lands,
  And sword, and fire and chains, and choice of harms.

  Medea superest, hic mare et terras uides
  ferrumque et ignes et deos et fulmina. (*Medea* 166-7.)

,,   Who now can heal
  My maimed mind? It must be heal'd by death.

    nemo polluto queat
  animo mederi. morte sanandum est scelus.
      (*Hercules Furens* 1268-9.)

,, Alone you may not die, with me you may.

  perire sine me non potes, mecum potes. (*Thebais* 66.)

,, They that will drive th' unwilling to their death,
  Or frustrate death in those that fain would die,
  Offend alike.

    qui cogit mori
  nolentem in aequo est quique properantem inpedit.
      (*Thebais* 98-99.)

,, ANG. But will my tears and mournings move you nought?
  GUEN. Then is it best to die when friends do mourn.

  THES.   lacrimae nonne te nostrae mouent?
  PHAE. mors optima est perire lacrimant dum sui.
      (*Hippolytus* 888-9.)

Page 270 Each-where is death! the fates have well ordain'd,
(continued). That each man may bereave himself of life,
But none of death: death is so sure a doom,
A thousand ways do guide us to our graves.

    ubique mors est. optume hoc cauit deus.
    eripere uitam nemo non homini potest,
    at nemo mortem: mille ad hanc aditus patent.
                             (*Thebais* 151-3.)

,, Who then can ever come too late to that,
Whence, when he is come, he never can return?
Or what avails to hasten on our ends,
And long for that which destinies have sworn!

    nemo ad id sero uenit unde numquam,
    cum semel uenit, potuit reuerti.
    quid iuuat dirum properare fatum?
                             (*Hercules Furens* 869-871.)

Page 271. Death is an end of pain, no pain itself.

    de fine poenae loquoris, ego poenam uolo. (*Thyestes* 246.)

,, Is 't meet a plague for such excessive wrong
Should be so short? Should one stroke answer all?
[*Soliloquizes*] And would'st thou die? well, that contents
    the laws:
What, then, for Arthur's ire? What for thy fame,
Which thou hast stain'd? What for thy stock thou
    sham'st?
Not death nor life can alone give a full
Revenge: join both in one—die and yet live.
Where pain may not be oft, let it be long.
Seek out some lingering death, whereby thy corpse
May neither touch the dead nor joy the quick.
Die, but no common death: pass nature's bounds,

> itane? tam magnis breues
> poenas sceleribus soluis atque uno omnia
> pensabis ictu? moreris: hoc patri sat est.
> quid deinde matri, quid male in lucem editis
> gnatis, quid ipsi quae tuum magna luit
> scelus ruina flebilis patriae dabis?
> soluenda non est illa quae leges ratas
> natura in uno uertit Oedipode nouos
> commenta partus, supplicis eadem meis
> nouetur. iterum uiuere atque iterum mori
> liceat renasci semper, ut totiens noua
> supplicia pendas. utere ingenio miser.
> quod saepe fieri non potest fiat diu.
> mors eligatur longa. quaeratur uia
> qua nec sepultis mixtus et uiuis tamen
> exemptus erres. morere sed citra patrem.
>   (*Oedipus* 957-972.)

Page 271 The mind and not the chance doth make th' unchaste.
(continued).
> mens inpudicam facere non casus solet. (*Hippolytus* 743.)

" Then is your fault from fate; you rest excus'd,
None can be deemed faulty for her fate.

> fati ista culpa est. nemo fit fato nocens. (*Oedipus* 1041.)

" Impute mishaps to fates, to manners faults.

> nam monstra fato, moribus scelera inputes.
>   (*Hippolytus* 149.)

" A mighty error oft hath seem'd a sin.

> saepe error ingens sceleris optinuit locum.
>   (*Hercules Furens* 1245.)

Page 272. The hour, which erst I always feared most
　　　　　 The certain ruin of my desperate state,
　　　　　 Is happened now! why turn'st thou (mind) thy back?
　　　　　 Why at the first assault dost thou recoil?
　　　　　 Trust to 't, the angry heavens contrive some spite,
　　　　　 And dreadful doom t' augment thy cursed hap.
　　　　　 Oppose to each revenge thy guilty head.

　　　　　　　　　quod tempus animo semper ac mente horrui,
　　　　　 adest profecto rebus extremum meis.
　　　　　 quid terga uertis anime? quid primo impetu
　　　　　 deponis arma? crede perniciem tibi
　　　　　 et dira saeuos fata moliri deos.
　　　　　 oppone cunctis uile suppliciis caput. (*Agamemnon* 227-232.)

Page 273. What shouldst thou fear, that see'st not what to hope?

　　　　　 qui nil potest sperare, desperet nihil.　　(*Medea* 163.)

　　　　　 cui ultima est fortuna, quid dubium timet?
　　　　　　　　　　　　　　　　　(*Agamemnon* 147.)

　,,　　　He safely stands, that stands beyond his harms.

　　　　　　　　　cuius haud ultra mala
　　　　　 exire possunt in loco tuto est situs.　　(*Thebais* 108-9.)

　,,　　　Thine (death) is all that east and west can see:
　　　　　 For thee we live, our coming is not long:
　　　　　 Spare us but whiles we may prepare our graves.
　　　　　 Though thou wert slow, we hasten of ourselves,
　　　　　 The hour that gave did also take our lives.

　　　　　　　　　tibi crescit omne,
　　　　　 et quod occasus uidet et quod ortus.
　　　　　 parce uenturis. tibi mors paramur.
　　　　　 sis licet segnis, properamus ipsi.
　　　　　 prima quae uitam dedit hora, carpit.
　　　　　　　　　　　　　　(*Hercules Furens* 874-8.)

Page 273   My fear is past, and wedlock love hath won.
(continued). Retire we thither yet, whence first we ought
Not to have stirr'd.   Call back chaste faith again.
The way that leads to good is ne'er too late :
Who so repents is guiltless of his crimes.

amor iugalis uincit ac flectit retro.
remeemus illuc, unde non decuit prius
abire.   sed nunc casta repetatur fides.
nam sera numquam est ad bonos mores uia.
quem paenitet pecasse, poenae est innocens.
(Agamemnon 240-244.)

Page 274.   Nor love nor sovereignty can bear a peer.

nec regna socium ferre nec taedae sciunt.
(Agamemnon 260.)

" Why dost thou still stir up my flames delay'd ?
His strays and errors must not move my mind :
A law for private men binds not the king.
What, that I ought not to condemn my liege,
Nor can, thus guilty to mine own offence !
Where both have done amiss, both will relent :
He will forgive that needs must be forgiven.

Aegisthe quid me rursus in praeceps rapis
iramque flammis iam residentem excitas?
permisit aliquid uictor in captam sibi :
nec coniugem hoc respicere nec dominam decet.
lex alia solio est alia priuato toro.
quid quod seueras ferre me leges uiro
non patitur animus turpis admissi memor.
det ille ueniam facile cui uenia est opus.
(Agamemnon 261-8.)

Page 274   A judge severe to us, mild to himself.
(continued).

           nobis maligni iudices aequi sibi.   (*Agamemnon* 271.)

"   His is the crime, whom crime stands most in stead.

                  cui prodest scelus,
     is fecit.   (*Medea* 503-4.)

"   Well should she seem most guiltless unto thee,
         Whate'er she be, that's guilty for thy sake.

     tibi innocens sit quisquis est pro te nocens.   (*Medea* 506.)

Page 275.   His ways be blind that maketh chance his guide.

     caeca est temeritas quae petit casum ducem.
                                  (*Agamemnon* 146.)

"   The safest passage is from bad to worse.

     per scelera semper sceleribus tutum est iter.
                                  (*Agamemnon* 116.)

"   He is a fool that puts a mean in crimes.

     res est profecto stulta nequitiae modus.   (*Agamemnon* 151.)

"   So sword and fire will often sear the sore.

     et ferrum et ignis saepe medicinae loco est.
                                  (*Agamemnon* 153.)

"   Extremest cures must not be used first.

     extrema primo nemo temptauit loco.   (*Agamemnon* 154.)

Page 275 (continued). In desperate times the headlong way is best.

capienda rebus in malis praeceps uia est.
(*Agamemnon* 155.)

Page 276. Mischief is sometimes safe, but ne'er secure,

scelus aliqua tutum, nulla securum tulit. (*Hippolytus* 169.)

  Con. The wrongful sceptre's held with trembling hand.
  Mor. Whose rule wants right, his safety's in his sword.

    rapta sed trepida manu
  sceptra optinentur.   omnis in ferro est salus.
     (*Hercules Furens* 345-6.)

"   Con. The kingliest point is to affect but right.
  Mor. Weak is the sceptre's hold that seeks but right.

  Sat. rex uelit honesta: nemo non eadem uolet.
  Atr. ubicumque tantum honesta dominanti licent,
  precario regnatur.   (*Thyestes* 213-5.)

Page 277. Mor. She is both light and vain.
  Con. She noteth though.
  Mor. She feareth states.
  Con. She carpeth, ne'ertheless.
  Mor. She's soon suppress'd.

  Sen. leuis atque uana.
  Nero.   sit licet, multos notat.
  Sen. excelsa metuit.
  Nero.   non minus carpit tamen.
  Sen. facile opprimetur.   (*Octavia* 596-8.)

Page 282. Con. Nought should be rashly vow'd against your sire.
Mor. Whose breast is free from rage may soon b' advised.
Con. The best redress from rage is to relent.
Mor. 'Tis better for a king to kill his foes.

Sen. in nihil propinquos temere constitui decet.
Nero. iustum esse facile est cui uacat pectus metu.
Sen. magnum timoris remedium clementia est.
Nero. extinguere hostem maxima est uirtus ducis.
(*Octavia* 452-5.)

Page 283. Con. The subjects' force is great.
Mor   Greater the king's.

Nvtr. uis magna populi est.
Oct.   principis maior tamen.
(*Octavia* 190.)

,,   The more you may, the more you ought to fear.

hoc plus uerere quod licet tantum tibi.   (*Octavia* 462.)

,,   Mor. He is a fool that feareth what he may.
Con. Not what you may, but what you ought is just.

Nero. inertis est nescire quid liceat sibi.
Sen. id facere laus est quod decet, non quod licet.
(*Octavia* 465-6.)

,,   Mor. The laws do licence as the soveleign lists.
Con. Least ought he list, whom laws do licence most.

Pyr. quodcumque libuit facere uictori, licet.
Agam. minimum decet libere cui multum licet.
(*Troas* 344-5.)

Page 283 MOR. The fates have heav'd and rais'd my force on high.
(continued). CON. The gentler should you press those that are low.

                quoque te celsum altius
        superi leuarunt, mitius lapsos preme. (*Troas* 704-5.)

Page 284. MOR. My will must go for right.
        CON.   If they assent.
        MOR. My sword shall force assent.
        CON.   No, gods forbid!

        NERO. statuam ipse.
        SEN.   quae consensus efficiat rata.
        NERO. despectus ensis faciet.
        SEN.   hoc absit nefas. (*Octavia* 472-3.)

     "   Whom fates constrain, let him forego his bliss;
        But he that needless yields unto his bane,
        When he may shun, doth well deserve to lose
        The good he cannot use.

        quem fata cogunt hic quidem uiuat miser,
        at si quis ultro se malis offert uolens
        seque ipse torquet, perdere est dignus bona
        quis nescit uti.   (*Hippolytus* 448-451.)

Page 285. Nor to destroy the realm you seek to rule.
        Your father rear'd it up, you pluck it down.
        You lose your country, whiles you win it thus:
        To make it yours, you strive to make it none.

                      ne precor ferro erue
        patriam ac penates neue, quas regere expetis
        euerte Thebas.   quis tenet mentem furor?
        petendo patriam perdis? ut fiat tua,
        uis esse nullam?   (*Thebais* 555-9.)

Page 285   Must I to gain renown incur my plague,
(continued).   Or hoping praise sustain an exile's life? [1]

       ut profugus errem semper? ut patria arcear
       opemque gentis hospes externae sequar?   (*Thebais* 586-7.)

,,   No. 'Tis my hap that Britain serves my turn;
     That fear of me doth make the subjects crouch;
     That what they grudge they do constrained yield.

       munus deorum est ipsa quod seruit mihi
       Roma et senatus quodque ab inuitis preces
       humilesque uoces exprimit nostri metus.   (*Octavia* 504-6.)

,,   Then is a kingdom at a wished stay,
     When whatsoever the sovereign wills or nills,
     Men be compell'd as well to praise as bear.

                maximum hoc regni bonum est,
       quod facta domini cogitur populus sui
       quam ferre tam laudare.   (*Thyestes* 205-7.)

---

[1] These lines have the following pasted over them:—
  The first art in a kingdom is to scorn
  The envy of the realm.

  ars prima regni est posse te inuidiam pati.
                         (*Hercules Furens* 357.)

                   He cannot rule
  That fears to be envi'd. What can divorce
  Envy from sovereignty?

  regnare non uult esse qui inuisus timet.
  simul ista mundi conditor posuit deus
  odium atque regnum.   (*Thebais* 654-6.)

Page 285. Con. But whoso seeks true praise and just renown,
Page 286. Would rather seek their praising hearts than tongues.
      Mor. True praise may happen to the basest groom ;
A forced praise to none but to a prince.
I wish that most, that subjects most repine.

      Sat. at qui fauoris gloriam ueri petit,
animo magis quam uoce laudari uolet.
      Atr. laus uera et humili saepe contingit uiro,
non nisi potenti falsa. quod nolunt, uelint.
(Thyestes 209-212.)

,, And better were an exile's life, than thus
Disloyally to wrong your sire and liege.

melius exilium est tibi
quam reditus iste.   *(Thebais* 617-8.)

,, But cease at length ; your speech molests me much.
My mind is fix'd : give Mordred leave to do
What Conan neither can allow nor like.

desiste tandem iam grauis nimium mihi
instare. liceat facere quod Seneca improbat.
(Octavia 600-601.)

Page 288. No danger can be thought both safe and oft.

nemo se tuto diu
periculis offerre tam crebris potest.
(Hercules Furens 330-331.)

,, Whom chance hath often miss'd, chance hits at length.

quem saepe transit casus aliquando inuenit.
(Hercules Furens 332.)

Page 289.   If conquerors ought
          To seek for peace, the conquered must perforce.

          pacem reduci uelle uictori expedit,
          uicto necesse est.   (*Hercules Furens* 372-3.)

"   What cursed wars (alas) were those, wherein
          Both son and sire should so oppose themselves!
          Him whom you now, unhappy man, pursue,
          If you should win, yourself would first bewail.

                    quale tu id bellum putas,
          in quo execrandum uictor admittit nefas
          si gaudet? hunc quem uincere infelix cupis
          cum uiceris, lugebis.   (*Thebais* 638-641.)

Page 290. Trust me, a huge and mighty kingdom 'tis
          To bear the want of kingdom, realm, and crown.

          immane regnum est posse sine regno pati. (*Thyestes* 470.)

"   Wherefore think on the doubtful state of wars.
          Where war hath sway, he keeps no certain course:
          Sometimes he lets the weaker to prevail,
          Sometimes the stronger troops: hope, fear, and rage
          With eyeless lot rules all uncertain good,
          Most certain harms be his assured haps.

          fortuna belli semper ancipiti in loco est.
          quodcumque Mars decernit: exaequat duos
          licet inpares sint gladius et spes et metus
          sors caeca uersat. praemium incertum petit,
          certum scelus.   (*Thebais* 629-633.)

"   Gaw. And fear you not so strange and uncouth wars?
          Mor. No, were they wars that grew from out the ground!

          Nvtr. non metuis arma?
          Med.   sint licet terra edita. (*Medea* 169.)

Page 290 (continued). He falleth well, that falling fells his foe.

    felix iacet, quicumque, quos odit, premit.
                                (*Hercules Oetaeus* 353.)

Page 291. Small manhood were to turn my back to chance.

    haud est uirile terga fortunae dare.   (*Oedipus* 86.)

,, I bear no breast so unprepar'd for harms.

    non inparatum pectus aerumnis gero.   (*Hippolytus* 1003.)

,, Even that I hold the kingliest point of all,
To brook afflictions well: and by how much
The more his state and tottering empire sags,
To fix so much the faster foot on ground.

        regium hoc ipsum reor
  aduersa capere quoque sit dubius magis
  status et cadentis imperi moles labat
  hoc stare certo pressius fortem gradu.   (*Oedipus* 82-85.)

,, No fear but doth forejudge, and many fall
Into their fate, whiles they do fear their fate.

  multis ipsum timuisse nocet.
  multi ad fatum uenere suum,
  dum fata timent.   (*Oedipus* 1014-16.)

,, Yea, worse than war itself is fear of war.

  peior est bello timor ipse belli.   (*Thyestes* 572.)

,, All things are rul'd in constant course: no fate
But is foreset: the first day leads the last.

  omnia certo tramite uadunt
  primusque dies dedit extremum.   (*Oedipus* 1008-9.)

Page 292. He either must destroy, or be destroy'd :
The mischief's in the midst; catch he that can.

    aut perdet, aut peribit, in medio est scelus
positum occupanti.   (*Thyestes* 203-4.)

,,   Like as the craggy rock
Resists the streams and flings the waltering waves
Aloof, so he rejects and scorns my words.

    ut dura cautes undique intractabilis
resistit undis et lacessentes aquas
longe remittit, uerba sic spernit mea.
    (*Hippolytus* 588-590.)

Page 295. A troubled head : my mind revolts to fear,
And bears my body back.

    nunc contra in metus
reuoluor, animus haeret ac retro cupit
corpus referre.   (*Thyestes* 418-420.)

Page 298. O false and guileful life. O crafty world !
Page 299. How cunningly convey'st thou fraud unseen !
Th' ambitious seemeth meek, the wanton chaste ;
Disguised vice for virtue vaunts itself.

    o uita fallax. obditos sensus geris
animisque pulcram turbidis faciem induis.
pudor inpudentem celat audacem quies,
pietas nefandum.   (*Hippolytus* 926-9.)

,,   No place is left for prosperous plight : mishaps
Have room and ways to run and walk at will.

    prosperis rebus locus
ereptus omnis, dira qua ueniant habent.   (*Troas* 432-3.)

Page 302.   Death only frees the guiltless from annoys.

      mors innocentem sola fortunae eripit.   (*Oedipus* 955.)

,,   Who so hath felt the force of greedy fates,
And 'dur'd the last decree of grisly death,
Shall never yield his captive arms to chains,
Nor drawn in triumph deck the victor's pomp.

    quisquis sub pedibus fata rapacia
et puppem posuit liminis ultimi,
non captiua dabit bracchia uinculis
nec pompae ueniet nobile ferculum.
                       (*Hercules Oetaeus* 107-110.)

,,   My youth (I grant) and prime of budding years,
Puff'd up with pride and fond desire of praise,
Foreweening nought what perils might ensue,
Adventured all and raught to will the reins:
But now this age requires a sager course,
And will, advis'd by harms, to wisdom yields.
Those swelling spirits, the self-same cause which first
Set them on gog, even fortune's favours quail'd.

    fateor aliquando inpotens
regno ac superbus altius memet tuli,
sed fregit illos spiritus haec quae dare
potuisset alii causa fortunae fauor.   (*Troas* 275-8.)

Page 303.   'Tis safest then to dare, when most you fear.

    tutissimum est inferre cum timens gradum.
                           (*Hippolytus* 730.)

,,   CADOR.   Then may you rule.
ARTHUR.   When I may die.
CADOR.   To rule is much.
ARTHUR.   Small, if we covet nought.

TANT. pater, potes regnare.
THY. cum possim mori.
TANT. summa est potestas.
THY. nulla si cupias nihil.
(*Thyestes* 442-3.)

Page 304. Trust me, bad things have often glorious names.

mihi crede, falsis magna nominibus placent.
(*Thyestes* 446.)

Page 305. Rome puffs us up, and makes us too—too fierce.
There, Britons, there we stand, whence Rome did fall.

Troia nos tumidos facit
nimium ac feroces? stamus hoc Danai loco
unde illa cecidit. (*Troas* 273-5.)

,, Thou, Lucius, mak'st me proud, thou heav'st my mind:
But what? Shall I esteem a crown ought else
Than as a gorgeous crest of easeless helm,
Or as some brittle mould of glorious pomp,
Or glittering glass which, while it shines, it breaks?
All this a sudden chance may dash, and not
Perhaps with thirteen kings, or in nine years:
All may not find so slow and lingering fates.

tu me superbum Priame tu tumidum facis.
ego esse quicquam sceptra nisi uano putem
fulgore tectum nomen et falso comam
uinclo decentem? casus haec rapiet breuis
nec mille forsan ratibus aut annis decem.
non omnibus fortuna tam lenta inuinet.
(*Troas* 279-284.)

Page 311. A hopeless fear forbids a happy fate.

miserrimum est timere cum speres nihil. (*Troas* 434.)

Page 311 All truth, all trust, all blood, all bands be broke!
(continued).
        fratris et fas et fides
iusque omne pereat.   (*Thyestes* 47-48.)

Page 312. For were it light, that ev'n by birth myself
        Was bad, I made my sister bad: nay, were
        That also light, I have begot as bad.

            hoc leue est quod sum nocens,
feci nocentes. hoc quoque etiamnunc leue est,
peperi nocentes.   (*Thebais* 367-9.)

Page 313. Care upon care, and every day a new
        Fresh rising tempest tires the tossed minds.

    alia ex aliis cura fatigat
uexatque animos noua tempestas. (*Agamemnon* 62-6?.)

  ,,   Who strives to stand in pomp of princely port.
        On giddy top and culm of slippery court,
        Finds oft a heavy fate; whiles too much known
        To all he falls unknown unto himself.

    stet quicumque uolet potens
    aulae culmine lubrico:
    ...   .
    illi mors grauis incubat,
    qui notus nimis omnibus,
    ignotus moritur sibi.   (*Thyestes* 391-2, 401-3.)

  ,,   My slender bark shall creep anenst the shore,
        And shun the winds that sweep the waltering waves.
        Proud fortune overslips the safest roads,
Page 314. And seeks amidst the surging seas those keels,
        Whose lofty tops and tacklings touch the clouds.

>   stringat tenuis litora puppis
>   nec magna meos aura phaselos
>   iubeat medium scindere pontum.
>   transit tutos fortuna sinus
>   medioque rates quaerit in alto
>   quarum feriunt suppara nubes.
>   (*Hercules Oetaeus* 698-703.)

Page 314 (*continued*).   With endless cark in glorious courts and towns,
The troubled hopes and trembling fears do dwell.

> turbine magno spes sollicitae
> urbibus errant trepidique metus.   (*Hercules Furens* 163-4.)

Page 315.   Who forbiddeth not offence,
If well he may, is cause of such offence.

> qui non uetat peccare, cum possit, iubet.   (*Troas* 300.)

Page 317.   Declare! we joy to handle all our harms.

> prosequere: gaudet aerumnas meus dolor
> tractare totas.   (*Troas* 1076-7.)

,,   Small griefs can speak, the great astonish'd stand.

> curae leues loquuntur ingentes stupent.   (*Hippolytus* 615.)

,,   GIL.   What greater sin could hap, than what be pass'd?
What mischiefs could be meant, more than were
    wrought?
NUN.   And think you there's to be an end to sins?
    No; crime proceeds: those made but one degree.

> CHOR.   an ultra maius aut atrocius
>   natura recipit?
> NVNT.   sceleris hunc finem putas?
>   gradus est.   (*Thyestes* 745 7.)

Page 325. He was the joy and hope, and hap, of all,
          The realm's defence, the sole delay of fates ;
          He was our wall and fort : twice thirteen years
          His shoulders did the Briton state support.

          columen patriae mora fatorum
          tu praesidium Phrygibus fessis
          tu murus eras umerisque tuis
          stetit illa decem fulta per annos.   (*Troas* 128-131.)

Page 332. Where each man else hath felt his several fate,
          I only pine, oppress'd with all their fates !

          sua quemque tantum, me omnium clades premit.
                                             (*Troas* 1071.)

Page 333. The hot-spurr'd youth, that forc'd the forward steeds,
          Whiles needs he would his father's chariot guide,
          Neglecting what his sire had said in charge :
          The fires which first he flung about the poles,
          Himself at last, most woful wretch, inflam'd.

          ausus aeternos agitare currus
          immemor metae iuuenis paternae
          quos polo sparsit furiosus ignes
          ipse recepit.   (*Medea* 602-605.)

Page 334. We could not join our minds—our fates we join'd.

          non licuit animos iungere, at certe licet
          iunxisse fata.   (*Hippolytus* 1192-3)

    ,,   They lov'd to live that, seeing all their realm
          Thus topsy-turvy turn, would grudge to die.

          uitae est auidus quisquis non uult
          mundo secum pereunte mori.   (*Thyestes* 886-7.)

Page 339. Whoe'er received such favour from above,
           That could assure one day unto himself?

           nemo tam diuos habuit fauentes,
           crastinum ut possit sibi polliceri. (*Thyestes* 619-620.)

    ,,   Him whom the morning found both stout and strong,
           The evening left all grovelling on the ground.

           quem dies uidit ueniens superbum,
           hunc dies uidit fugiens iacentem. (*Thyestes* 613-4.)

GUARDIAN STEAM PRINTING WORKS, OXFORD STREET, BOLTON.

www.ingramcontent.com/pod-product-compliance
Lightning Source LLC
Chambersburg PA
CBHW030305170426
43202CB00009B/883